Lee Kuan Yew

The Belfer Center Studies in International Security book series is edited at the Belfer Center for Science and International Affairs at the Harvard Kennedy School and is published by The MIT Press. The series publishes books on contemporary issues in international security policy, as well as their conceptual and historical foundations. Topics of particular interest to the series include the spread of weapons of mass destruction, internal conflict, the international effects of democracy and democratization, and U.S. defense policy. A complete list of Belfer Center Studies appears at the back of this volume.

Lee Kuan Yew

The Grand Master's Insights on China, the United States, and the World

Interviews and Selections by
Graham Allison and Robert D. Blackwill
with Ali Wyne

Foreword by Henry A. Kissinger

BELFER CENTER STUDIES IN INTERNATIONAL SECURITY
The MIT Press
Cambridge, Massachusetts
London, England

Library of Congress Cataloging-in-Publication Data

Lee, Kuan Yew, 1923–
[Interviews. Selections]
Lee Kuan Yew : the grand master's insights on China, the United States, and the world / interviews and selections by Graham Allison and Robert D. Blackwill ; with Ali Wyne ; foreword by Henry A. Kissinger.
    p.   cm. — (Belfer center studies in international security)
Includes bibliographical references and index.
ISBN 978-0-262-01912-5 (hardcover : alk. paper)
1. World politics. I. Allison, Graham T. II. Blackwill, Robert D. III. Wyne, Ali, 1987– IV. Title.
D31.L44   2013
303.4909'0512—dc23

                                                                            2012032250

10   9   8   7

Contents

Foreword

I have had the privilege of meeting many world leaders over the past half century; none, however, has taught me more than Lee Kuan Yew, Singapore's first premier and its guiding spirit ever since. As to the ancient argument—whether individuals shape events or are their register—there can be no doubt about the answer with regard to Lee Kuan Yew, a man of unmatched intelligence and judgment.

By far the smallest country in Southeast Asia, Singapore seemed destined to become a client state of more powerful neighbors, if indeed it could preserve its independence at all. Lee thought otherwise. His vision was of a state that would not simply survive, but prevail by excelling. Superior intelligence, discipline, and ingenuity would substitute for resources. He summoned his compatriots to a duty that they had never previously perceived: first to clean up their city, then to dedicate it to overcome the initial hostility of their neighbors and their own ethnic divisions by superior performance. The Singapore of today is his testament.

When Lee took over, per capita income was about $400 a year; it is now more than $50,000. He inspired his polyglot population to become the intellectual and technical center of the Asia-Pacific. Because of his leadership, a medium-sized city has become a significant international and economic player, especially in fostering multilateral transpacific ties.

Along the way, Lee has made himself an indispensable friend of the United States, not primarily by the power he represents, but by the excellence of his thinking. His analysis is of such quality and depth that his counterparts consider meeting with him as a way to educate themselves. For three generations now, whenever Lee comes to Washington, he meets with an array of people spanning the top ranks of the American government and foreign policy community. His discussions occur in an atmosphere of rare candor borne of high regard and long-shared experience. Every American president who has dealt with him has benefited from the fact that, on international issues, he has identified the future of his country with the fate of the democracies. Furthermore, Lee can tell us about the nature of the world that we face, with especially penetrating insights into the thinking of his region.

Lee's analyses shed light on the most important challenge that the United States confronts over the long term: how to build a fundamental and organic relationship with Asia, including China. There is nobody who can teach us more about the nature and the scope of this effort than Lee Kuan Yew. As this book demonstrates, however, his insights extend far beyond U.S.-China relations; they encompass virtually every challenge of international relations. It will not take long for readers to discover why Lee is not only one of the seminal leaders of our period, but also a thinker recognized for his singular strategic acumen.

—*Henry A. Kissinger*
New York, April 2012

Who Is Lee Kuan Yew?

A strategist's strategist

A leader's leader

A mentor's mentor

When Lee Kuan Yew Talks, Who Listens?

Presidents

Barack Obama, president of the United States

Lee "is one of the legendary figures of Asia in the 20th and 21st centuries. He is somebody who helped to trigger the Asian economic miracle." (October 29, 2009)

Bill Clinton, 42nd president of the United States

"Lee's life of public service is both unique and remarkable. . . . His work as Prime Minister and now as Minister Mentor has helped literally millions of people in Singapore and all across Southeast Asia to live better, more prosperous lives. I hope the leaders of ASEAN [the Association of Southeast Asian Nations] will continue to build upon Mr. Lee Kuan Yew's outstanding legacy. . . . I thank you [the U.S.-ASEAN Business Council] for honoring a man I admire so very much." (October 27, 2009)

George H. W. Bush, 41st president of the United States

"In my long life in public service, I have encountered many bright, able people. None is more impressive than Lee Kuan Yew." (endorsement of Lee's *My Lifelong Challenge: Singapore's Bilingual Journey*, 2011)

Jacques Chirac, president of France (1995–2007)

"Lee Kuan Yew has gathered around himself the most brilliant minds, transforming the most exacting standards into a system of government. Under his leadership, the primacy of the general interest, the cult of education, work and saving, and the capacity to foresee the needs of the city have enabled Singapore to take what I call 'shortcuts to progress.'" (endorsement of Lee's *From Third World to First: The Singapore Story: 1965–2000*, 2000)

F. W. de Klerk, president of South Africa (1989–94)

"The leader who, perhaps, impressed me most was Lee Kuan Yew of Singapore. . . . He was an individual who changed the course of history. . . . Lee Kuan Yew took the right decisions for his country; he chose the right values and the right economic policies to ensure the development of a successful society. In this, he was an artist painting on the largest canvas that society can provide. He was also a very astute judge of the world and provided a very canny and realistic assessment of our situation in South Africa when I met him during the early nineties." (March 30, 2012)

Chinese Leaders

Xi Jinping, likely incoming president of China

Lee is "our senior who has our respect": "To this day, you are still working tirelessly to advance our bilateral relationship, and you have my full admiration. We will never forget the important contribution you have made to our bilateral relationship." (May 23, 2011)

Other Heads of Government

Tony Blair, prime minister of the United Kingdom (1997–2007)

Lee is "the smartest leader I think I ever met." (Blair, *A Journey: My Political Life*, 2010)

John Major, prime minister of the United Kingdom (1990–97)

"Lee Kuan Yew can justifiably be called the father of modern Singapore. He has steered through policies that have been copied across Asia, and have greatly lifted the profile and representation of Singapore. It is a legacy that will endure." (comment in Tom Plate's *Conversations with Lee Kuan Yew: Citizen Singapore: How to Build a Nation*, 2010)

Margaret Thatcher, prime minister of the United Kingdom (1979–90)

"In office, I read and analyzed every speech of Lee's. He had a way of penetrating the fog of propaganda and expressing with unique clarity the issues of our times and the way to tackle them. He was never wrong." (endorsement of Lee's *From Third World to First: The Singapore Story: 1965–2000*, 2000)

Helmut Schmidt, chancellor of Germany (1974–82)

"Ever since I met my friend Lee Kuan Yew, I was highly impressed by his brilliant intellect and his straight overview. His lifetime achievements as a political leader and statesman are outstanding. The economic and social advancement of modern Singapore is deeply rooted in his capability to establish an adequate political framework for Singapore's ethnical heterogeneity. This book is yet another proof of his perspicacity and competence." (endorsement of Lee's *My Lifelong Challenge: Singapore's Bilingual Journey*, 2011)

Heads of Global Corporations and Economic Institutions

Rupert Murdoch, chairman and chief executive officer of News Corporation

"More than 40 years ago, Lee Kuan Yew transformed what was a poor, decrepit colony into a shining, rich, and modern metropolis—all the time surrounded by hostile powers. With his brilliant, incisive intellect, he is one of the world's most outspoken and respected statesmen. This book is a 'must read' for any student of modern Asia." (endorsement of Lee's *From Third World to First: The Singapore Story: 1965–2000*, 2000)

John Chambers, chairman and chief executive officer of Cisco Systems

"There are two equalizers in life: the Internet and education. Lee Kuan Yew is a world leader who understands this and is using the power of the Internet to position Singapore for survival and success in the Internet economy." (endorsement of Lee's *From Third World to First: The Singapore Story: 1965–2000*, 2000)

Sam Palmisano, chairman of IBM

"It is terrific to be at the Lee Kuan Yew School of Public Policy. It is especially special for me because a gentleman I admire so much, and have learned so much from, is Minister Mentor Lee Kuan Yew. He has given me lots of tutelage on Asia and China and India, and has tremendous insights." (February 1, 2011)

Rex Tillerson, chairman, president, and chief executive officer of Exxon Mobil

"For so many years, you [addressing Lee] have been a willing mentor to leaders of government, business, and for me personally. The Ford's Theatre Lincoln Medal is given to individuals who . . . exemplify the lasting legacy and mettle of character embodied by President Abraham Lincoln. Few leaders in modern history meet these criteria more than tonight's honoree. . . . Abraham Lincoln once said . . . 'Towering genius disdains a beaten path.' For the people of Singapore, Lee Kuan Yew was such a towering leader who held a bold vision for his nation. He did not lead them down the beaten path of narrow-minded protectionism, but down the broad avenues of global engagement and economic competitiveness." (October 18, 2011)

Robert Zoellick, president of the World Bank (2007–12)

"As soon as I learned a number of years ago about the Lee Kuan Yew School, I wanted to figure out some way to at least come by. I cannot think of a better testament for a leader who has made a huge mark in the world." (December 18, 2008)

James Wolfensohn, president of the World Bank (1995–2005)

"I used to be the adviser to the Minister Mentor. It was a very hard job because I traveled to Singapore, and every time I was just about to tell something to Mr. Minister Mentor, he would stop me and tell me the thing I was to tell him. Then I would return to the United States and sell his advice. Thank you very much, Mr. Minister Mentor, for all the things you have taught me. I tried giving you my advice. But, in fact, it was you who taught me." (July 10, 2007)

Muhtar Kent, chairman and chief executive officer of Coca-Cola

"History will record few leaders who have accomplished so much for their country and for Southeast Asia as His Excellency Lee Kuan Yew. As a driving force behind the growth and evolution of ASEAN, Mr. Lee also helped millions of people across Southeast Asia to live in an environment of peace and economic growth." (October 27, 2009)

David Rothkopf, president and chief executive officer of Garten Rothkopf

"Like many other visitors, you wonder whether this tiny island [Singapore] that did not even exist as a truly independent nation until 1965 is perhaps the best-run city in the world, whether maybe the ancient Greeks and Singapore's founder, Lee Kuan Yew, were on to something when they settled on the idea of city-states. . . . During the course of the half century in which he has led Singapore, he has emerged as one of the world's most effective if sometimes controversial leaders." (Rothkopf, *Power, Inc.*, 2012)

Senior Policymakers

Hillary Clinton, U.S. secretary of state

"I am delighted to welcome the Minister Mentor here [to the White House] today. . . . Singapore is a long and valued partner on so many important issues. And I think it is fair to say, sir [addressing Lee], that you have a great many admirers. You are here to accept an important award [the U.S.-ASEAN Business Council's Lifetime Achievement Award] that is given for lifetime achievement, and I join in the many Americans who thank you for your service." (October 26, 2009)

George Shultz, U.S. secretary of state (1982–89)

"You [addressing Lee] have taught all of us a tremendous amount by what you have done, what you have said, [and] the way you mean it when you say something, and I thank you." (October 27, 2009)

Madeleine Albright, U.S. secretary of state (1997–2001)

"He has the most modern and most strategic view of anyone I have met for a long time." (July 30, 1997)

Zbigniew Brzezinski, U.S. national security adviser (1977–81)

"He is among the most intellectually alert of the world's leaders. . . . He is capable of expatiating at length and with perception on virtually any international problem; he is a most astute observer of the Asian scene; and he is candid in passing along to us Asian perceptions of our changing role in that part of the world." (September 16, 1977)

Larry Summers, director of the U.S. National Economic Council (2009–10) and U.S. secretary of the Treasury (1999–2001)

"It is more than a little bit daunting to be talking about the subject of governance just before Lee Kuan Yew speaks." (September 15, 2006)

xxii   *Lee Kuan Yew*

Robert Rubin, U.S. secretary of the Treasury (1995–99)

"Lee is deeply knowledgeable about geopolitical and cultural matters. . . . I had gotten to know the Senior Minister somewhat during the Asian financial crisis, when he had demonstrated the enormous depth of his geopolitical understanding and grasp of regional issues." (Rubin, *In an Uncertain World: Tough Choices from Wall Street to Washington*, with Jacob Weisberg, 2003)

Joseph Nye, chairman of the U.S. National Intelligence Council (1993–94)

"Today, it [Singapore] is a rich and prosperous country. If the rest of the world could accomplish what Singapore has accomplished, the world would be a better and more prosperous place. . . . He is a man who never stops thinking, never stops looking ahead with larger visions. His views are sought by respected senior statesmen on all continents." (October 17, 2000)

Commentators

Nicholas Kristof, opinion columnist for the New York Times

"Other leaders have reshaped nations—Kemal Ataturk in Turkey, Lenin in Russia, Deng Xiaoping in China—but no one left a deeper imprint on his people than Lee. . . . One can disagree with him, but intolerance and authoritarianism have never had so articulate or stimulating a spokesman. These [*From Third World to First*] are rich memoirs, the legacy of an extraordinary man, and in many ways, this book is like Lee himself: smart, thoughtful, blunt, and provocative." (November 5, 2000)

David Ignatius, opinion columnist for the Washington Post

"He is probably the smartest politician I have interviewed in more than 25 years as a journalist." (September 28, 2002)

Fareed Zakaria, editor-at-large of Time

"Lee Kuan Yew took a small spit of land in Southeast Asia, which became independent in 1965 after great struggle and anguish, with no resources and a polyglot population of Chinese, Malaysian, and Indian workers, and turned it into one of the economic centers of the world. To do this, Lee had to have smart economic policies, but also a shrewd foreign policy. . . . He is still indisputably the father of Singapore. I was struck by the depth of his understanding of the world—China, Russia, and the United States—all at age 85." (September 21, 2008)

Preface

Lee Kuan Yew is unique among statesmen of the past half century. The "founding father" and dominant figure in Singapore for more than five decades, he took a poor, corrupt city-state and built a modern nation whose citizens now have incomes higher than those of most Americans. Not only as a thinker, but also as a primary actor, he knows about transformation.

In international affairs, no individual has been more eagerly sought out, more regularly consulted, and more carefully listened to by a generation of American, Chinese, and other world leaders than the "sage of Singapore." From Richard Nixon and Henry Kissinger, when they were designing the "opening to China" in 1971–72, to every occupant of the White House since, American presidents, including Barack Obama, have gone out of their way to stop in Singapore and have welcomed Lee to the Oval Office when he visits

the United States. From Deng Xiaoping, when he first began con-
templating a radical march to a market-based economy that would
ignite three decades of double-digit growth; to Hu Jintao and the
likely incoming president, Xi Jinping, Lee has been their most influential counselor outside of China.

Beyond the great powers, smaller states such as Israel, whose
survival depends on being alert to trends beyond their borders,
have found in Lee a source of insight and inspiration. From
Kazakhstan's Nursultan Nazarbayev, when he found himself the
leader of a newly independent country that had never existed, to
the United Arab Emirates' Sheikh Khalifa bin Zayed, to Rwanda's
Paul Kagame, and scores of others, leaders with great challenges
have found in Lee strategic coordinates that help them navigate
their international challenges.

The purpose of this slim volume is not to look back on the past
50 years, remarkable as Lee's contributions to them have been.
Rather, our focus is the future and the specific challenges that
the United States will face during the next quarter century. We have
tried to imagine the questions that the individual who takes the
presidential oath of office on January 20, 2013, would find of most
immediate interest, and then to summarize Lee's most direct responses in his own words. We are confident that these answers will
be of value not only to those shaping American foreign policy, but
also to leaders of businesses and civil society in the United States,
who are making investments of scarce dollars and even scarcer time

based on their expectations about significant trends in the wider world. We are grateful to Anthony Tan and Yeong Yoon Ying for facilitating our interviews with Lee.

The ten chapters that follow begin with the rise of China, the issue about which Lee undoubtedly knows more than any other outside observer or analyst. Will China challenge America's position as the leading power in Asia, and in time the world? Most policymakers and pundits answer this central question with a combination of fog and abstractions. Cutting through that cant and caution, Lee answers: "Of course. Their reawakened sense of destiny is an overpowering force. It is China's intention to be the greatest power in the world—and to be accepted as China, not as an honorary member of the West."

We then ask about the United States and the U.S.-China relationship that will shape international politics in the 21st century. Between these two great powers, Lee sees confrontation: "There will be a struggle for influence. Competition between them is inevitable." But contrary to pessimistic realists, he does not judge conflict inevitable if leaders of both nations exercise reasonable judgment.

Successive chapters address India, Islamic extremism, geopolitics and globalization, and democracy, among other topics. Each chapter starts with key questions and then offers a succinct summary of Lee's answers. Many of those answers have an edge, since he has congenitally pushed back against "political correctness" and never shrunk from controversy. As authors and architects of this book, we have resisted the temptation to comment or offer our own views, mindful that presidents and their closest advisers will most benefit from Lee's counsel, not ours.

We have extracted Lee's key insights and central arguments so that they can be scanned quickly. Make no mistake: we believe that every word on every page that follows deserves to be read, but readers can make that judgment for themselves. We suspect that those hoping to make a quick dash through the book will find themselves spending more time than they expected, compelled by Lee's words to pause and think about assertions of his that they find surprising, even disturbing, but invariably illuminating.

The opportunity to spend many hours listening to Lee and poring over his voluminous writings, interviews, and speeches has been more fulfilling than we could have ever expected. If we can offer readers a taste of that banquet, we will have fulfilled our aspirations.

CHAPTER 1

The Future of China

Are Chinese leaders serious about displacing the United States as the number 1 power in Asia? In the world? What does number 1 mean? How will China's behavior toward other countries change if China becomes the dominant Asian power? What is China's strategy for becoming number 1? What are the major hurdles in executing that strategy? How much urgency do China's leaders feel about achieving primacy in their region and beyond? How do China's leaders see the U.S. role in Asia changing as China becomes number 1? Is the double-digit growth that China has maintained over three decades likely to continue for the next several decades? Will China become a democracy? Will China actually become number 1? How should one assess Xi Jinping? These questions are central to the likely course of Asian and world history. Lee Kuan Yew's thoughtful answers in this chapter reflect decades of observing and analyzing China and its leaders.

Are Chinese leaders serious about displacing the United States as the number 1 power in Asia? In the world?

Of course. Why not? They have transformed a poor society by an economic miracle to become now the second-largest economy in the world—on track, as Goldman Sachs has predicted, to become the world's largest economy in the next 20 years. They have followed the American lead in putting people in space and shooting down satellites with missiles. Theirs is a culture 4,000 years old with 1.3 billion people, many of great talent—a huge and very talented pool to draw from. How could they not aspire to be number 1 in Asia, and in time the world?[1]

Today, China is the world's fastest developing nation, growing at rates unimaginable 50 years ago, a dramatic transformation no one predicted. . . . The Chinese people have raised their expectations and aspirations. Every Chinese wants a strong and rich China, a nation as prosperous, advanced, and technologically competent as America, Europe, and Japan. This reawakened sense of destiny is an overpowering force.[2]

The Chinese will want to share this century as co-equals with the U.S.[3]

It is China's intention to be the greatest power in the world. The policies of all governments toward China, especially neighboring countries, have already taken this into account. These governments are repositioning themselves because they know that there will be consequences if they thwart China when its core interests are at stake. China can impose economic sanctions simply by denying access to its market of 1.3 billion people, whose incomes and purchasing power are increasing.[4]

Unlike other emergent countries, China wants to be China and accepted as such, not as an honorary member of the West.[5]

What does number 1 mean? How will China's behavior toward other countries change if China becomes the dominant Asian power?

At the core of their mindset is their world before colonization and the exploitation and humiliation that brought. In Chinese, China means "Middle Kingdom"—recalling a world in which they were dominant in the region, other states related to them as supplicants to a superior, and vassals came to Beijing bearing tribute: for example, the sultan of Brunei, who carried silk as his offering, but who died there four centuries ago and now has a shrine in Beijing.[6]

Will an industrialized and strong China be as benign to Southeast Asia as the United States has been since 1945? Singapore is not sure. Neither are Brunei, Indonesia, Malaysia, the Philippines,

Thailand, and Vietnam. . . . We already see a China more self-assured and willing to take tough positions.[7]

The concern of America is what kind of world they will face when China is able to contest their preeminence. . . . Many medium and small countries in Asia are also concerned. They are uneasy that China may want to resume the imperial status it had in earlier centuries and have misgivings about being treated as vassal states having to send tribute to China as they used to in past centuries.[8]

They expect Singaporeans to be more respectful of China as it grows more influential. They tell us that countries big or small are equal: we are not a hegemon. But when we do something they do not like, they say you have made 1.3 billion people unhappy. . . . So please know your place.[9]

What is China's strategy for becoming number 1?

The Chinese have concluded that their best strategy is to build a strong and prosperous future, and use their huge and increasingly highly skilled and educated workers to out-sell and out-build all others. They will avoid any action that will sour up relations with the U.S. To challenge a stronger and technologically superior power like the U.S. will abort their "peaceful rise."[10]

China is following an approach consistent with ideas in the Chinese television series *The Rise of Great Powers,* produced by the Party to shape discussion of this issue among Chinese elites. The mistake of Germany and Japan was their effort to challenge the existing order. The Chinese are not stupid; they have avoided this mistake. . . . Overall GDP [gross domestic product], not GDP per capita, is what matters in terms of power. . . . China will not reach the American level in terms of military capabilities anytime soon, but is rapidly developing asymmetrical means to deter U.S. military power. China understands that its growth depends on imports, including energy, raw materials, and food. . . . China also needs open sea lanes. Beijing is worried about its dependence on the Strait of Malacca and is moving to ease the dependence.[11]

The Chinese have calculated that they need 30 to 40, maybe 50, years of peace and quiet to catch up, build up their system, change it from the communist system to the market system. They must avoid the mistakes made by Germany and Japan. Their competition for power, influence, and resources led in the last century to two terrible wars. . . . The Russian mistake was that they put so much into military expenditure and so little into civilian technology. So their economy collapsed. I believe the Chinese leadership has learnt that if you compete with America in armaments, you will lose. You will bankrupt yourself. So, avoid it, keep your head down, and smile, for 40 or 50 years.[12]

To become competitive, China is focused on educating its young people, selecting the brightest for science and technology, followed by economics, business management, and the English language.[13]

My first reaction to the phrase "peaceful rise" was to tell one of their think tanks, "It is a contradiction in terms; any rise is something that is startling." And they said, "What would you say?" I replied: "Peaceful renaissance, or evolution, or development." A recovery of ancient glory, an updating of a once great civilization. But it is already done. Now the Chinese have to construe it as best they can. A year ago, a Chinese leader in his 70s asked me, "Do you believe our position on peaceful rise?" I answered, "Yes, I do—but with one caveat." Your generation has been through the anti-Japanese war, the Great Leap Forward, the Cultural Revolution, the Gang of Four, and finally the Open Door policy. You know there are many pitfalls, that for China to go up the escalator without mishaps, internally you need stability, externally you need peace. However, you are inculcating enormous pride and patriotism in your young in a restored China. . . . It is volatile." The Chinese leader said they would ensure that the young understood. Well, I hope they do. Somewhere down this road, a generation may believe they have come of age, before they have.[14]

China's strategy for Southeast Asia is fairly simple: China tells the region, "come grow with me." At the same time, China's leaders want to convey the impression that China's rise is inevitable and that countries will need to decide if they want to be China's friend or foe when it "arrives." China is also willing to calibrate its engagement to get what it wants or express its displeasure.[15]

China is sucking the Southeast Asian countries into its economic system because of its vast market and growing purchasing power. Japan and South Korea will inevitably be sucked in as well. It just absorbs countries without having to use force. China's neighbors want the U.S. to stay engaged in the Asia-Pacific so that they are not hostages to China. The U.S. should have established a free-trade area with Southeast Asia 30 years ago, well before the Chinese magnet began to pull the region into its orbit. If it had done so, its purchasing power would now be so much greater than it is, and all of the Southeast Asian countries would have been linked to the U.S. economy rather than depending on China's. Economics sets underlying trends. China's growing economic sway will be very difficult to fight.[16]

China's emphasis is on expanding their influence through the economy. In the geopolitical sense, they are more concerned now with using diplomacy in their foreign policy, not force.[17]

What are the major hurdles in executing that strategy?

Internally, the chief challenges are culture, language, an inability to attract and integrate talent from other countries, and, in time, governance.[18]

Even if China were as open to talented immigrants as the U.S., how can one go there and integrate into society without a mastery of Chinese? Chinese is a very difficult language to learn— monosyllabic and tonal. One can learn conversational Chinese after a few years, but it is very difficult to be able to read quickly.

I do not know if China will be able to overcome the language barrier and the attendant difficulty in recruiting outside talent unless it makes English the dominant language, as Singapore has.

Children there learn Chinese first. Then they learn English. They might go to the U.S. as a teenager and become fluent, but they have 4,000 years of Chinese epigrams in their head.[19]

China will inevitably catch up to the U.S. in absolute GDP. But its creativity may never match America's, because its culture does not permit a free exchange and contest of ideas. How else to explain how a country with four times as many people as America—and presumably four times as many talented people—does not come up with technological breakthroughs?[20]

Can the Chinese break free from their own culture? It will require going against the grain of 5,000 years of Chinese history. When the center is strong, the country prospers. When the center is weak, the emperor is far away, the mountains are high, and there are many little emperors in the provinces and counties. This is their cultural heritage. . . . Chinese traditions thus produce a more uniform mandarinate.[21]

The biggest single fear China's leaders have is the corrosive effect of graft and the revulsion that it evokes in people. They are never quite sure when it will blow up.[22]

There will be enormous stresses because of the size of the country and the intractable nature of the problems, the poor infrastructure, the weak institutions, the wrong systems that they have installed, modeling themselves upon the Soviet system in Stalin's time.[23]

China faces enormous economic problems—a disparity in income between the rich coastal cities and the inland provinces, and in income within the coastal cities. They have got to watch that carefully or they might get severe discontent and civil disorder.[24]

Technology is going to make their system of governance obsolete. By 2030, 70% or maybe 75% of their people will be in cities, small towns, big towns, mega big towns. They are going to have cell phones, Internet, satellite TV. They are going to be well-informed; they can organize themselves. You cannot govern them the way you are governing them now, where you just placate and monitor a few people, because the numbers will be so large.[25]

Increasingly cheap and available technology and cascades of reverse migration are wising people up to the true story of the exploitation of China's heretofore isolated rural regions. And, furthermore, the Chinese know that with their industrialization, every year, ten or plus millions will go into the new towns they are constructing for their people. . . . If they change in a pragmatic way, as they have been doing, keeping tight security control and not allowing riots and not allowing rebellions and, at the same time, easing up . . . giving more provincial authority, more city authority, more grassroots power, it is holdable.[26]

China did not have to worry about the rest of the world when it was an empire. This time, it has to worry about the rest of the world, because without the resources, the oil, the nickel, whatever, its growth will stop.[27]

Present-day China faces a very advanced North America, Europe, Japan, and a fairly developed Southeast Asia and India. . . . China's leaders 30 years hence will know that although by 2050

China will be the biggest economy in GNP [gross national product], per capita, they will still be small, and technologically, they will still be way behind. So to get there, they must have a sense of realism. . . . They have got to be like Singapore's leaders, with a very keen sense of what is possible and what is not. They must know that to dominate Asia is not possible.[28]

Straight-line extrapolations from such a remarkable record are not realistic. China has more handicaps going forward and more obstacles to overcome than most observers recognize. Chief among these are their problems of governance: the absence of the rule of law, which in today's China is closer to the rule of the emperor; a huge country in which little emperors across a vast expanse exercise great local influence; cultural habits that limit imagination and creativity, rewarding conformity; a language that shapes thinking through epigrams and 4,000 years of texts that suggest everything worth saying has already been said, and said better by earlier writers; a language that is exceedingly difficult for foreigners to learn sufficiently to embrace China and be embraced by its society; and severe constraints on its ability to attract and assimilate talent from other societies in the world.

While Singapore shares with China many of the core philosophical tenets of Confucianism, we worked over the past 40 years to establish English as our first language, and Chinese as the second. Why? Certainly not by accident or without provoking strong opposition. We did so to open ourselves to the world and allow ourselves to engage and embrace the main forces of discovery and invention and creativity that occur not only in the language but also in the mentality of English.

We could do that in a small city-state with strong leadership. While I once advised a Chinese leader to make English the first language of China, clearly that is not realistic for such a great, confident country and culture. But it is a serious handicap.[29]

How much urgency do China's leaders feel about achieving primacy in their region and beyond?

The Chinese are in no hurry to displace the U.S. as the number 1 power in the world and to carry the burden that is part and parcel of that position. For now, they are quite comfortable in being part of a larger group like the G20 [Group of Twenty] where their views will be taken seriously and economic interests safeguarded, but the responsibility is shared amongst 20 member states.[30]

While there are no doubt voices calling for China to move more rapidly in establishing its superiority, demanding the respect that comes along with that standing, and exercising this role, the center of gravity among the leaders is cautious and conservative. They operate on the basis of consensus and have a long view. While some may imagine that the 21st century will belong to China, others expect to share this century with the U.S. as they build up to China's century to follow.[31]

How do China's leaders see the U.S. role in Asia changing as China becomes number 1?

The leadership recognizes that as the leading power in the region for the seven decades since World War II, the U.S. has provided a stability that allowed unprecedented growth for many nations including Japan, the Asian Tigers, and China itself. China knows that it needs access to U.S. markets, U.S. technology, opportunities for Chinese students to study in the U.S. and bring back to China new ideas about new frontiers. It therefore sees no profit in confronting the U.S. in the next 20 to 30 years in a way that could jeopardize these benefits.

Rather, its strategy is to grow within this framework, biding its time until it becomes strong enough to successfully redefine this political and economic order.

In the security arena, the Chinese understand that the U.S. has spent so much more and has built up such advantages that direct challenges would be futile. Not until China has overtaken the U.S. in the development and application of technology can they envisage confronting the U.S. militarily.[32]

What are the Americans going to fight China over? Control over East Asia? The Chinese need not fight over East Asia. Slowly and gradually, they will expand their economic ties with East Asia and offer them their market of 1.3 billion consumers. . . . Extrapolate that another 10, 20 years and they will be the top importer and exporter of all East Asian countries. How can the Americans compete in trade?[33]

I do not see the Americans retreating from Asia. But I see Chinese power growing. The Chinese attitude is: we are not against you; we welcome an American presence—because they know they cannot substitute for the Americans, and the countries here welcome the Americans. So they just wait and grow stronger. Economically and militarily, they may not catch up for 100 years in technology, but asymmetrically, they can inflict enormous damage on the Americans.[34]

Is the double-digit growth that China has maintained over three decades likely to continue for the next several decades?

During the last three decades, China's economy has grown at the phenomenal rate of 10% per year, sometimes even exceeding 12%. Can China maintain such high rates for at least another decade? I think it can. China is starting from a lower base, and its 1.3 billion domestic consumers will keep rates up because their disposable incomes are growing.[35]

Will China become a democracy?

No. China is not going to become a liberal democracy; if it did, it would collapse. Of that, I am quite sure, and the Chinese intelligentsia also understands that. If you believe that there is going to be a revolution of some sort in China for democracy, you are wrong. Where are the students of Tiananmen now? They are irrelevant. The Chinese people want a revived China.[36]

Can it be a parliamentary democracy? This is a possibility in the villages and small towns. . . . The Chinese fear chaos and will always err on the side of caution. It will be a long evolutionary process, but it is possible to contemplate such changes. Transportation and communications have become so much faster and cheaper. The Chinese people will be exposed to other systems and cultures and know other societies through travel, through the Internet, and through smart phones. One thing is for sure: the present system will not remain unchanged for the next 50 years.[37]

To achieve the modernization of China, her Communist leaders are prepared to try all and every method, except for democracy with one person and one vote in a multi-party system. Their two main reasons are their belief that the Communist Party of China must have a monopoly on power to ensure stability; and their deep fear of instability in a multiparty free-for-all, which would lead to a loss of control by the center over the provinces, with horrendous consequences, like the warlord years of the 1920s and '30s.[38]

I do not believe you can impose on other countries standards which are alien and totally disconnected with their past. So to ask China to become a democracy, when in its 5,000 years of recorded history it never counted heads; all rulers ruled by right of being the emperor, and if you disagree, you chop off heads, not count heads.

But I agree that in this world of instant communication and satellites, you cannot have barbaric behavior and say it is your internal problem. . . . But now on human rights, they have begun to talk, and they recognize that if they want to be respected in the world community, they want to win a certain status with the rest of the world, not just advanced countries, but even the developing countries, then they cannot behave in a barbaric fashion to their own people.[39]

(In 1993, Lee offered a vision of Chinese governance in 2150.)[40] China discovered that to run a modern state it needed the rule of law. It had a comprehensive set of legal codes by 2035 and found that a stable legal system, together with clear administrative rules, actually strengthened central authority. Erring provincial and local governments were brought to book through due process of law, a method more effective than the endless negotiations that had been the practice before. Also, with the rule of law, ordinary citizens are now protected from the arbitrary authority of officials. Business enterprises are also able to plan large long-term investments. The independence of the judiciary took another 20 years to achieve in practice, because historical tradition, which required magistrates, as officers of the emperor, to carry out imperial orders, was deeply embedded in Chinese officialdom.

Will China actually become number 1?

Their great advantage is not in military influence but in their economic influence. . . . They have the manpower to do things cheaper in any part of the world economically. Their influence can only grow and grow beyond the capabilities of America.[41]

The chances of it going wrong in China—if they have pragmatic, realistic leaders who are not ideologically blinkered—are about one in five. I would not say zero, because their problems are weighty ones: system change, business culture change, reducing corruption, and forming new mindsets.[42]

The Chinese have figured out that if they stay with "peaceful rise" and just contest for first position economically and technologically, they cannot lose.[43]

The 21st century will see Asia recover its place in the world. Their progress in the last 30 years entitles East Asians including the Chinese to be optimistic about their future. Short of some major unforeseeable disaster which brings chaos or breaks up China once again into so many warlord fiefdoms, it is only a question of time before the Chinese people reorganize, reeducate, and train themselves to take full advantage of modern science and technology. China will quicken the pace of its development by using inputs from the industrial and newly industrializing countries to catch up with and become, first, a fully industrialized, and next, a high-tech society—if not in 50 years, then in 100 years.[44]

How should one assess Xi Jinping [the likely incoming president of China]?

He has had a tougher life than Hu Jintao. His father was rusticated, and so was he. He took it in his stride, worked his way up the southern provinces quietly, and rose to become secretary of Fujian Province. Then he went to Shanghai, and then to Beijing. It has not been smooth sailing for him. His life experiences must have hardened him.

He is reserved—not in the sense that he will not talk to you, but in the sense that he will not betray his likes and dislikes. There is always a pleasant smile on his face, whether or not you have said something that annoyed him. He has iron in his soul, more than Hu Jintao, who ascended the ranks without experiencing the trials and tribulations that Xi endured.[45]

I would put him in Nelson Mandela's class of persons. A person with enormous emotional stability who does not allow his personal misfortunes or sufferings to affect his judgment. In other words, he is impressive.[46]

CHAPTER 2

The Future of the United States

Is the United States in systemic decline? What are America's primary strengths? What worries you about the U.S. government? What worries you about U.S. culture? Does effective governance require "guardians"? Is the United States at risk of becoming European? What does the U.S. need to do to maintain global primacy? In this chapter, Lee Kuan Yew draws on his long experience with the United States to offer perceptive and provocative answers to these questions.

19

Is the United States in systemic decline?

Absolutely not. The U.S. is going through a bumpy patch with its debt and deficits, but I have no doubt that America will not be reduced to second-rate status. Historically, the U.S. has demonstrated a great capacity for renewal and revival. America's strengths include no grooved thinking but rather an ability to range widely, imaginatively, and pragmatically; a diversity of centers of excellence that compete in inventing and embracing new ideas and new technologies; a society that attracts talent from around the world and assimilates them comfortably as Americans; and a language that is the equivalent of an open system that is clearly the lingua franca of the leaders in science, technology, invention, business, education, diplomacy, and those who rise to the top of their own societies around the world.[1]

Although America is currently facing tremendously difficult economic times, America's creativity, resilience, and innovative spirit will allow it to confront its core problems, overcome them, and regain competitiveness.[2]

For the next two to three decades, America will remain the sole superpower. The U.S. is the most militarily powerful and economically dynamic country in the world. It is the engine for global growth through its innovation, productivity, and consumption.[3]

Today and for the next few decades, it is the U.S. that will be preeminent in setting the rules of the game. No major issue concerning international peace and stability can be resolved without U.S. leadership, and no country or grouping can yet replace America as the dominant global power.[4]

The U.S. response to the terrorist attacks of 9/11 demonstrated America's preeminence. That shock altered the attitudes of Americans on how to deal with terrorist threats to their society. Washington did not hesitate to use its enormous power to change the rules of the game to hunt down and destroy terrorists and those who give them succor.[5]

For the next few decades, the U.S. will be a virtual American empire. Whether you are African or South American or Indian or Filipino or Chinese or Korean, Americans will let you work for them in America and in their multinational corporations abroad. . . . Throughout history, all empires that succeeded have embraced and included in their midst people of other races, languages, religions, and cultures.[6]

For the next 10, 15, 20 years, the U.S. will remain the most enterprising, innovative economy because of its leading-edge technology, both in the civilian and military fields. . . . You will lose that gradually over 30, 40, 50 years unless you are able to keep on attracting talent, and that is the final contest, because the Chinese and other nations are going to adopt parts of what you have done to fit their circumstances, and they are also going around looking for talented people and building up their innovative, enterprising economies. And finally, this is now an age when you will not have military contests between great nations, because you will destroy each other, but you will have economic and technological contests between the great powers.[7]

What are America's primary strengths?

Americans have a can-do approach to life: everything can be broken up, analyzed, and redefined. Whether it can or it cannot, Americans believe it can be solved, given enough money, research, and effort. Over the years, I have watched the Americans revise and restructure their economy, after they were going down in the 1980s, when Japan and Germany looked like they were eclipsing America, taking over all the manufacturing. Americans came roaring back. They have the superior system. It is more competitive.[8]

What has made the U.S. economy preeminent is its entrepreneurial culture. . . . Entrepreneurs and investors alike see risk and failure as natural and necessary for success. When they fail, they pick themselves up and start afresh. The Europeans and the Japanese now have the task of adopting these practices to increase their efficiency and competitiveness. But many American practices go against the grain of the more comfortable and communitarian cultural systems of their own societies—the Japanese with life-long employment for their workers, the Germans with their unions having a say in management under co-determination, and the French with their government supporting the right of unions to pressure businesses from retrenching, by requiring large compensation to be paid to laid-off workers.[9]

The U.S. is a frontier society. . . . There is a great urge to start new enterprises and create wealth. The U.S. has been the most dynamic society in innovating, in starting up companies to commercialize new discoveries or inventions, thus creating new wealth. American society is always on the move and changing. . . . For every successful entrepreneur in America, many have tried and failed. Quite a few tried repeatedly until they succeeded. Quite a few who succeeded continued to create and start up new companies as serial entrepreneurs. . . . This is the spirit that generates a dynamic economy.[10]

The American culture . . . is that we start from scratch and beat you. That is why I have confidence that the American economy will recover. They were going down against Japan and Germany in manufacturing. But they came up with the Internet, Microsoft and Bill Gates, and Dell. . . . What kind of mindset do you need for that? It is part of their history. They went into an empty continent and made the best of it—killed the Red Indians and took over the land and the buffaloes. So this is how they ended up—you build a town here, you be the sheriff, I am the judge, you are the policeman, and you are the banker, let us start. And this culture has carried on until today. There is the belief that you can make it happen.[11]

The Americans have succeeded as against the Europeans and the Japanese because they have more extremes of random behavior. You have the mean, you have the bell curve, and you have two extreme ends. And the more you have of the extreme ends on the good side, the more creativity and inventiveness you have.[12]

One fundamental difference between American and Oriental culture is the individual's position in society. In American culture, an individual's interest is primary. This makes American society more aggressively competitive, with a sharper edge and higher performance.[13]

The Americans will always have the advantage because of their all-embracive society, and the English language that makes it easy to attract foreign talent. America has a clear advantage over China, because its use of the English language enables America to attract millions of English-speaking foreign talent from Asia and Europe. There is an off chance that the United States will lose confidence in itself, will not be so creative, so inventive, and creating breakthroughs in new technologies and not attracting new talents from abroad. I do not see the United States in the next 10, 20, 30 years losing that capability. Talent will not go to China. Talent will go to America because Americans speak English and everybody fits in. It is a country that embraces immigrants. To go and settle in China, you have to master the Chinese language. And you must get used to the Chinese culture. And that is a very difficult hurdle to clear.[14]

The U.S. is the only superpower because of its advances in science and technology and their contribution to its economic and military might.[15]

The U.S. dollar is likely to remain the leading currency, because the American economy will remain the most entrepreneurial and dynamic in the world.[16]

America is a great nation not just because of its power and wealth, but mainly because it is a nation moved by high ideals. Only the elevating power of her idealism can explain the benign manner in which America has exercised its enormous power since the end of World War II and the magnanimity and generosity with which it has shared its wealth to rebuild a more prosperous world.[17]

The United States is the most benign of all the great powers, certainly less heavy-handed than any emerging great power. . . . As long as its economy leads the world, and America stays ahead in innovation and technology, neither the European Union nor Japan nor China can displace the United States from its present pre-eminent position.[18]

What worries you about the U.S. government?

When you have popular democracy, to win votes you have to give more and more. And to beat your opponent in the next election, you have to promise to give more away. So it is a never-ending process of auctions—and the cost, the debt being paid for by the next generation.[19]

Presidents do not get reelected if they give a hard dose of medicine to their people. So, there is a tendency to procrastinate, to postpone unpopular policies in order to win elections. So, problems such as budget deficits, debt, and high unemployment have been carried forward from one administration to the next.[20]

If the President and the Congress are conscribed by popular sentiment, then they will always be captive. America must have leaders who are prepared to lead and know what is good for America and do it, even if they lose their reelection. A system of governance that does not allow them to do a quiet U-turn when they identify problems is malfunctioning.[21]

A certain coyness or diffidence seems to have descended on American politicians. American academics and journalists freely discuss America's problems and weaknesses. But in the years since the Vietnam War ended, the American voter has shown a disinclination to listen to their political leaders when they debate the hard issues. Perhaps for this reason, neither the Republican nor the Democratic Party has focused on the urgent need to cut down deficit spending, especially on welfare, to increase savings and investments, or, most crucial of all, to improve America's school system to produce workers who are able to compete internationally.[22]

The presidential system is less likely to produce good government than a parliamentary system. In the presidential system, your personal appearance on TV is decisive, whereas in a parliamentary system, the prime minister, before he becomes the prime minister, has been a member of parliament, and probably a minister, and in Britain the people have sized you up over a period of time . . . and they have come to certain conclusions as to what kind of a person you are, what kind of depth you have, what kind of sincerity you have in what you say. . . . Your presidents, I mean, like Jimmy Carter . . . my name is Jimmy Carter, I am a peanut farmer, I am running for president. The next thing you know, he was the president![23]

Security, prosperity, and the consumer society plus mass communications have made for a different kind of person getting elected as leader, one who can present himself and his programs in a polished way. . . . I am amazed at the way media professionals can give a candidate a new image and transform him, at least superficially, into a different personality. Winning an election becomes, in large measure, a contest in packaging and advertising. . . . A spin doctor is a high-income professional, one in great demand. From such a process, I doubt if a Churchill, a Roosevelt, or a de Gaulle can emerge.[24]

Contrary to what American political commentators say, I do not believe that democracy necessarily leads to development. I believe that what a country needs to develop is discipline more than democracy. The exuberance of democracy leads to undisciplined and disorderly conditions which are inimical to development. The ultimate test of the value of a political system is whether it helps that society to establish conditions which improve the standard of living for the majority of its people, plus enabling the maximum of personal freedoms compatible with the freedoms of others in society.[25]

One problem is the Philippines has an American-style constitution, one of the most difficult to operate in the world. There is a complete separation of powers between the executive, legislature, and judiciary. . . . But a developing country faced with disorder and underdevelopment needs a strong, honest government. . . . I do not believe that Korea, Taiwan, Hong Kong, or Singapore could have succeeded . . . if they had to work under such a constitution, where gridlock on every major issue is a way of life. And you will notice that since the Vietnam War and the Great Society . . . the U.S. system has not functioned even for the United States.[26]

Americans seem to think that Asia is like a movie and that you can freeze developments out here whenever the U.S. becomes intensely involved elsewhere in the world. It does not work like that. If the United States wants to substantially affect the strategic evolution of Asia, it cannot come and go.[27]

I would like to believe that you can discern your interests dispassionately so as not to have the pendulum swing away from Asia because of your rather tiresome experiences in Vietnam. I accept the world as I find it. One thing I find is the disillusionment of the American people against the losses they have sustained.[28]

What worries you about U.S. culture?

I find parts of it totally unacceptable: guns, drugs, violent crime, vagrancy, unbecoming behavior in public, in sum, the breakdown of civil society. The expansion of the right of the individual to behave or misbehave as he or she pleases has come at the expense of orderly society. . . . It has a lot to do with the erosion of the moral underpinnings of a society and the diminution of personal responsibility. The liberal, intellectual tradition that developed after World

War II claimed that human beings had arrived at this perfect state where everybody would be better off if they were allowed to do their own thing and flourish. It has not worked out, and I doubt if it will. . . . There is already a backlash in America against failed social policies that have resulted in people urinating in public, in aggressive begging in the streets, in social breakdown. . . . You must have order in society. Guns, drugs, and violent crime all go together, threatening social order.[29]

The ideas of individual supremacy . . . when carried to excess, have not worked. They have made it difficult to keep American society cohesive. Asia can see it is not working. Those who want a wholesome society where young girls and old ladies can walk in the streets at night, where the young are not preyed upon by drug peddlers, will not follow the American model. . . . The top 3 to 5% of a society can handle this free-for-all, this clash of ideas. If you do this with the whole mass, you will have a mess. . . . To have, day to day, images of violence and raw sex on the picture tube, the whole society exposed to it, it will ruin a whole community.[30]

When Asians visit the U.S., many are puzzled and disturbed by conditions there: law and order out of control, with riots, drugs, guns, muggings, rape, and crimes; poverty in the midst of great wealth; excessive rights of the individual at the expense of the community as a whole; and criminals regularly escape punishment because the law which presumes innocence over-protects their human rights. . . . In the U.S., the community's interests have been sacrificed because of the human rights of drug traffickers and drug consumers. Drug-related crimes flourish. Schools are infected. There is high delinquency and violence amongst students, a high dropout rate, poor discipline and teaching, producing students who make poor workers. So a vicious cycle has set in.[31]

I do not believe that if you are libertarian, full of diverse opinions, full of competing ideas in the marketplace, full of sound and fury, therefore you will succeed.[32]

America's sense of cultural supremacy is again evident when the American media praises Taiwan, Korea, the Philippines, or Thailand for becoming democratic and having a free press. It is praise with condescension, compliments from a superior culture patting an inferior one on the head. And it is this same sense of cultural supremacy which leads the American media to pick on Singapore and beat us up as authoritarian, dictatorial; an over-ruled, over-restricted, stifling, sterile society. Why? Because we have not complied with their ideas of how we should govern ourselves. But we can ill afford to let others experiment with our lives. Their ideas are theories, theories not proven, not proven in East Asia, not even in the Philippines after they had governed the Philippines for 50 years. Nor are they proven as yet in Taiwan, or Thailand, or Korea.[33]

Multiculturalism will destroy America. There is a danger that large numbers of Mexicans and others from South and Central America will continue to come to the U.S. and spread their culture across the whole of the country. If they breed faster than the WASPs [white Anglo-Saxon Protestants] and are living with them, whose culture will prevail? Will the WASPs change them, or will the immigrants change the existing culture? They will change each other, but it would be sad for American culture to be changed even partially.[34]

Long term for America, if you project another 100 years, 150 years into the 22nd century, whether you stay on top depends upon the kind of society you will be, because if the present trends continue, you will have a Hispanic element in your society that is about 30, 40%. So, the question is, do you make the Hispanics Anglo-Saxons in culture or do they make you more Latin American in culture? . . . If they come in drips and drabs and you scatter them across America, then you will change their culture, but if they come in large numbers, like Miami, and they stay together, or in California, then their culture will continue, and they may well affect the Anglo-Saxon culture around them. That is the real test.[35]

I do not subscribe to the American or British style of politicking. I am not sure in Europe today whether they dig into your family affairs, but in America, they do. So they play up Michelle Obama, the children, the dogs, and so on. Maybe it gives them a better sense of the family, but how does that help them in deciding whether Obama is a good president and whether he is concentrating on the right things to get the economy going?[36]

Does effective governance require "guardians"?

For Singapore, the basic challenge remains unchanged: unless we have a steady stream of high-quality people to serve as PM [prime minister] and ministers, Singapore as a little red dot will become a little black spot. . . . To find able and committed people of integrity, willing to spend the prime of their lives, and going through the risky process of elections, we cannot underpay our ministers and argue that their sole reward should be their contribution to the public good.

We did not bring Singapore from the Third to the First World by head-hunting ministers willing to sacrifice their children's future when undertaking a public service duty. We took a pragmatic course that does not require people of caliber to give up too much for the public good. We must not reduce Singapore to another ordinary country in the Third World by dodging the issue of competitive ministerial remuneration.[37]

They say people can think for themselves? Do you honestly believe that the chap who cannot pass elementary school knows the consequences of his choice when he answers a question viscerally, on language, culture, and religion? But we knew the consequences. We would starve, we would have race riots. We would disintegrate.[38]

To get good government, you must have good people in charge of government. I have observed in the last 40 years that even with a poor system of government, but with good strong people in charge, people get passable government with decent progress. On the other hand, I have seen many ideal systems of government fail. Britain and France between them wrote over 80 constitutions for their different colonies. Nothing wrong with the constitution, with the institutions and the checks and the balances. But the societies did not have the leaders who could work those institutions, nor the people who respected those institutions. . . . The leaders who inherited these constitutions were not equal to the job, and their countries failed, and their system collapsed in riots, in coups, and in revolution.[39]

If a people have lost faith completely in their democratic institutions because they cannot find people of caliber to run them, however good that system, it perishes. Ultimately, it is the people who run the system who make it come to life.[40]

It is essential to rear a generation at the very top of society that has all the qualities needed to lead and give the people the inspiration and the drive to make it succeed. In short, the elite. . . . All those with the potential to blossom forth must do so. That is the spearhead in the society, on whom depends the pace of our progress.[41]

People in the mass can only govern themselves, and obtain their needs, either through traditional or through representative leaders. A well-ordered society with a long unbroken history, like Britain or Japan, has its national solidarity and its establishment based on the king and the royal family, a religion and the elders of the church, the elite in the ruling parties who alternate in power, the elite in the public service and the armed forces, the elite in commerce, industry, and in the professions.[42]

There is no better way to run the country than the best person for the most difficult job.[43]

Is the United States at risk of becoming European?

If you follow the ideological direction of Europe, you are done for. There will always be a tussle within societies, as underachievers want more support, but addressing their needs must be done in a way that does not kill incentive.[44]

American and European governments believed that they could always afford to support the poor and the needy: widows, orphans, the old and homeless, disadvantaged minorities, unwed mothers. Their sociologists expounded the theory that hardship and failure were due not to the individual person's character, but to flaws in the economic system. So charity became "entitlement," and the stigma of living on charity disappeared. Unfortunately, welfare costs grew faster than the government's ability to raise taxes to pay for it. The political cost of tax increases is high. Governments took the easy way out by borrowing to give higher benefits to the current generation of voters and passing the costs on to the future generation who were not yet voters. This resulted in persistent government budget deficits and high public debt.[45]

We would like Singaporeans to emulate this American self-help culture. This cultural trait has made Americans great entrepreneurs who have the verve, vitality, and vigor to keep adapting and changing their businesses, and therefore their economy, much better than Europeans or Japanese.[46]

If the U.S. becomes more like Europe, with a pretty widespread social security net, payment to the unemployed, Medicare is going to cost them an extra $1.2 trillion in ten years—I do not know where the money is going to come from—if the U.S. goes that way, it will become a slower economy even after private enterprise has taken over.[47]

What does the U.S. need to do to maintain global primacy?

The 21st century will be a contest for supremacy in the Pacific, because that is where the growth will be. That is where the bulk of the economic strength of the globe will come from. If the U.S. does not hold its ground in the Pacific, it cannot be a world leader.[48]

America's core interest requires that it remains the superior power on the Pacific. To give up this position would diminish America's role throughout the world.[49]

To hold ground in the Pacific, the U.S. must not let its fiscal deficits come to grief. If they come to grief and there is a run on the dollar for whatever reason . . . and the bankers and all the hedge funds and everybody come to a conclusion that the U.S. is not going to tackle these deficits, and they begin to move their assets out, that would spell real trouble. . . . America's debt is what worries me most, because it will absolutely strike at the heart of America's global leadership.[50]

The U.S. must not let its preoccupation with the Middle East—Iraq, Iran, the Israelis, and oil—allow others, especially China, to overtake its interests in Southeast Asia. The Chinese are not distracted. They are looking for energy everywhere, and they are making friends everywhere, including here.[51]

⊕

CHAPTER 3

The Future of U.S.-China Relations

How likely is a major confrontation between the United States and China? What role should the balance of power play in America's strategy for addressing the rise of China? How should U.S. policies and actions adjust to deal with the rise of China? What policies and actions should the United States avoid in dealing with the rise of China? Can U.S. policies and actions significantly influence China's trajectory and behavior as it emerges as a great power? How should Chinese policies and actions adjust to establish a sustained cooperative relationship with the United States? Managing a changing relationship with China is a central challenge of U.S. foreign policy in the 21st century. In his answers to these questions, Lee Kuan Yew offers his advice to U.S. leaders.

⊕

How likely is a major confrontation between the United States and China?

This is not the Cold War. The Soviet Union was contesting the U.S. for global supremacy. China is acting purely as China in its own national interests. It is not interested in changing the world.[1]

There will be a struggle for influence. I think it will be subdued because the Chinese need the U.S., need U.S. markets, U.S. technology, need to have students going to the U.S. to study ways and means of doing business so they can improve their lot. It will take them 10, 20, 30 years. If you quarrel with the U.S. and become bitter enemies, all that information and technological capabilities will be cut off. The struggle between the two countries will be maintained at the level that allows them to still tap the U.S.[2]

Unlike U.S.-Soviet relations during the Cold War, there is no irreconcilable ideological conflict between the U.S. and a China that has enthusiastically embraced the market. . . . Sino-U.S. relations are both cooperative and competitive. Competition between them is inevitable, but conflict is not.[3]

After the collapse of the Soviet Union, the U.S. and China are more likely to view each other as competitors if not adversaries. But the die has not been cast. The best possible outcome is a new understanding that when they cannot cooperate, they will coexist and allow all countries in the Pacific to grow and thrive.[4]

A stabilizing factor in their relationship . . . is that each nation requires cooperation from and healthy competition with the other. The danger of a military conflict between China and the U.S. is low. Chinese leaders know that U.S. military superiority is overwhelming, and will remain so for the next few decades. They will modernize their forces not to challenge America but to be able, if necessary, to pressure Taiwan by a blockade, or otherwise to destabilize the economy.[5]

China will not let an international court arbitrate territorial disputes in the South China Sea, so the presence of U.S. firepower in the Asia-Pacific will be necessary if the United Nations Law of the Sea is to prevail.[6]

What role should the balance of power play in America's strategy for addressing the rise of China?

Prudence dictates that there be a balance of power in the Asia-Pacific region. This is reflected in a widely held consensus that the U.S. presence in the region should be sustained. . . . A military presence does not need to be used to be useful. Its presence makes a difference, and makes for peace and stability in the region. This stability serves the interest of all, including that of China.[7]

Peace and security both in Europe and in the Pacific still depend on a balance of power. A U.S. military presence in both regions is very necessary. However, unless the U.S. economy becomes more dynamic and less debt-laden, this presence will be much reduced by the end of this decade [the 1990s]. The longer-term outlook then becomes problematic. Even if the U.S. deficits are reduced, industrial productivity improves, and exports increase, the U.S. nevertheless cannot afford and will not be willing to bear the whole cost of the global security burden. . . . The great danger is that the U.S. economy does not recover quickly enough, and trade frictions and Japan bashing increase as America becomes protectionist. The worst case is where trade and economic relations become so bad that mutual security ties are weakened and ruptured. That would be a dreadful and dangerous development.[8]

The world has developed because of the stability America established. If that stability is rocked, we are going to have a different situation.[9]

The size of China makes it impossible for the rest of Asia, including Japan and India, to match it in weight and capacity in about 20 to 30 years. So we need America to strike a balance.[10]

The question is whether the U.S. can continue its role as a key security and economic player in the Pacific. If she can, East Asia's future is excellent. But there will be problems if the U.S. economy does not recover its competitiveness within the next ten years.[11]

The U.S. cannot afford to abandon Japan unless it is willing to risk losing its leverage on both China and Japan. Whether or not there is an America-Japan Mutual Security Treaty, the only stable balance that can be maintained is a triangular one between Japan and the U.S. on the one side and China on the other. This is inevitable because of China's potential weight, which far exceeds that of the U.S. and Japan combined.[12]

Why should the U.S. stay engaged to help East Asia's combined GNP [gross national product] to exceed that of North America? Why not disengage and abort this process? Because this process is not easily aborted. It will be slowed or stalled for some years, but only until Japan, China, Korea, and the Russian Republic establish a new balance. However, no alternative balance can be as comfortable as the present one, with the U.S. as a major player. . . . The geopolitical balance without the U.S. as a principal force will be very different from that which it now is or can be if the U.S. remains a central player. My generation of Asians, who have experienced the last war, its horrors and miseries, and who remember the U.S. role in the phoenix-like rise from the ashes of that war to prosperity of Japan, the newly industrializing economies, and ASEAN [the Association of Southeast Asian Nations], will feel a keen sense of regret that the world will become so vastly different because the U.S. becomes a less central player in the new balance.[13]

President Nixon was a pragmatic strategist. He would engage, not contain, China, but he would also quietly set pieces into place for a fallback position should China not play according to the rules as a good global citizen. In such circumstances, where countries will be forced to take sides, he would arrange to win over to America's side of the chessboard Japan, Korea, ASEAN, India, Australia, New Zealand, and the Russian Federation.[14]

How should U.S. policies and actions adjust to deal with the rise of China?

For America to be displaced, not in the world, but only in the western Pacific, by an Asian people long despised and dismissed with contempt as decadent, feeble, corrupt, and inept is emotionally very difficult to accept. The sense of cultural supremacy of the Americans will make this adjustment most difficult. Americans believe their ideas are universal—the supremacy of the individual and free, unfettered expression. But they are not—never were. In fact, American society was so successful for so long not because of these ideas and principles, but because of a certain geopolitical good fortune, an abundance of resources and immigrant energy, a generous flow of capital and technology from Europe, and two wide oceans that kept conflicts of the world away from American shores.[15]

Americans have to eventually share their preeminent position with China.[16]

The U.S. cannot stop China's rise. It just has to live with a bigger China, which will be completely novel for the U.S., as no country has ever been big enough to challenge its position. China will be able to do so in 20 to 30 years.[17]

The size of China's displacement of the world balance is such that the world must find a new balance in 30 to 40 years. It is not possible to pretend that this is just another big player. This is the biggest player in the history of the world.[18]

The U.S. Congress is against any new free-trade agreements. If the next Congress continues to oppose FTAs, valuable time will be lost, and it may be too late to try again. Congress must be made to realize how high the stakes are and that the outlook for a balanced and equitable relationship between the American and Chinese markets is becoming increasingly difficult. Every year, China attracts more imports and exports from its neighbors than the U.S. does from the region. Without an FTA, Korea, Japan, Taiwan, and the ASEAN countries will be integrated into China's economy—an outcome to be avoided.[19]

What policies and actions should the United States avoid in dealing with the rise of China?

Do not treat China as an enemy from the outset. Otherwise, it will develop a counterstrategy to demolish the U.S. in the Asia-Pacific; in fact, it is already discussing such a strategy. There will inevitably be a contest between the two countries for supremacy in the western Pacific, but it need not lead to conflict.[20]

The baiting of China by American human rights groups, and the threatening of loss of most-favored-nation status and other sanctions by the U.S. Congress and administration for violations of human rights and missile technology transfers . . . ignore differences of culture, values, and history, and subordinate the strategic considerations of China-U.S. relations to an American domestic agenda. Such a haphazard approach risks turning China into a long-term adversary of the U.S. Less sensitivity and more understanding of the cultural realities of China can make for a less confrontational relationship.[21]

With the disintegration of the Soviet Union, U.S.-China relations are no longer anchored in a common threat. The U.S. has yet to settle on a bipartisan policy on China. China has the potential to become a superpower. America's interest is to maintain the status quo, where it is the only superpower, but in 30 years, China's growth could challenge this preeminence. . . . U.S. policy towards China has been driven by extraneous factors, like the saturation media coverage of Tiananmen, the plight of Chinese dissidents fleeing persecution, democracy, human rights, and most-favored-nation status, autonomy for Tibet and the Dalai Lama, and Taiwan seeking to become an independent United Nations member. . . . Issues which challenge China's sovereignty and unity will arouse China's hostility. To emphasize such issues makes sense only if it is U.S. policy to contain China and to slow down or abort its rapid economic growth.[22]

Massive economic reforms have opened up China. If liberalization is the goal of U.S. policy, then more trade and investments are the answers. Instead, the U.S. threatens to derail this process by cutting off most-favored-nation status. The State Department draws up its report on China's human rights like a headmaster drawing up a pupil's annual report for the parents. This may make Americans feel good and Chinese look small, but East Asians are uneasy over its long-term consequences.[23]

It is the U.S., more than any other country, that can integrate

China into the international community. . . . The difficulty arises from America's expressed desire to make China more democratic. China resents and resists this as interference in its domestic matters. Outside powers cannot refashion China into their own image. . . . American society is too pluralistic, its interests too varied to have a single or unanimous view of China. Sometimes the language of discourse in America has caused the Chinese to wonder if by engagement the U.S. does not mean an engagement in combat. . . . China has to be persuaded that the U.S. does not want to break up China before it is more willing to discuss questions of world security and stability.[24]

Can U.S. policies and actions significantly influence China's trajectory and behavior as it emerges as a great power?

Yes indeed. If the U.S. attempts to humiliate China, keep it down, it will assure itself an enemy. If instead it accepts China as a big, powerful, rising state and gives it a seat in the boardroom, China will take that place for the foreseeable future. So if I were an American, I would speak well of China, acknowledge it as a great power, applaud its return to its position of respect and restoration of its glorious past, and propose specific concrete ways to work together.[25]

Why should the U.S. take on China now when it knows that doing so will create an unnecessary adversary for a very long time—and one that will grow in strength and will treat it as an enemy? It is not necessary. The U.S. should say: We will eventually be equal, and

you may eventually be bigger than me, but we have to work together. Have a seat, and let us discuss the world's problems."[26]

This is the fundamental choice that the United States has to
make: to engage or to isolate China. You cannot have it both ways.
You cannot say you will engage China on some issues and isolate
her over others. You cannot mix your signals.[27]

America's greatest long-term influence on China comes from
playing host to the thousands of students who come from China
each year, some of the ablest of Chinese scholars and scientists.
They will be the most powerful agents for change in China.[28]

As China's development nears the point when it will have
enough weight to elbow its way into the region, it will make a fateful
decision—whether to be a hegemon, using its economic and military weight to create a sphere of influence . . . or to continue as a
good international citizen. . . . It is in everyone's interest that before
that moment of choice arrives, China should be given every incentive to choose international cooperation which will absorb its ener-
gies constructively for another 50 to 100 years. This means China
must have the economic opportunities to do this peacefully, without having to push its way to get resources like oil, and have access to markets for its goods and services. . . . If such a route is not
open to China, the world must live with a pushy China. . . . The
United States can through dialogue and cooperation with China
chart a course to manage China's transition in the next 20–30 years
into a big power. . . . China is an old civilization and will not easily
change because of external pressure or sanctions. But changes will

come when their leaders, thinkers, and intellectuals become convinced on their own that adopting certain attributes and features of other societies will benefit China.[29]

The best way to quicken the pace and direction of political change in China is to increase her trade and investment links with the world. Then her prosperity will depend increasingly on the compatibility of her economic system with those of the major trading nations. And wide-ranging contacts will influence and modify her cultural values and moral standards.[30]

Integrating China into the global system will build up strong vested interests in China to play by international rules. It will increase China's interdependence for trade, services, investments, technology, and information. These interdependent links could increase to a point where to break them in a unilateral breach of international obligations would carry unbearable costs.[31]

Peace and security in the Asia-Pacific will turn on whether China emerges as a xenophobic, chauvinistic force, bitter and hostile to the West because it tried to slow down or abort its development, or educated and involved in the ways of the world, more cosmopolitan, more internationalized and outward-looking.[32]

How should Chinese policies and actions adjust to establish a sustained cooperative relationship with the United States?

From 1945 to 1979, China was engaged in a series of wars that nearly broke them. . . . This generation has been through hell: the

Great Leap Forward, hunger, starvation, near collision with the Russians . . . the Cultural Revolution gone mad. . . . I have no doubt that this generation wants a peaceful rise. But the grandchildren? They think that they have already arrived, and if they begin to flex their muscles, we will have a very different China. . . . Grandchildren never listen to grandfathers. The other problem is a more crucial one: if you start off with the belief that the world has been unkind to you, the world has exploited you, the imperialists have devastated you, looted Beijing, done all this to you . . . this is no good. . . . You are not going back to old China, when you were the only power in the world as far as you knew. . . . Now, you are just one of many powers, many of them more innovative, inventive, and resilient. . . . If I were America, Europe, or Japan, I would spend time to make sure that the mindset of the younger generation is not one of hostility, but one of acceptance and an understanding that you are now a stakeholder, which was Bob Zoellick's very apt description of their role. . . . Make them feel that they are stakeholders, and if this earth goes warm, they will be in as much trouble as anyone else.[33]

It is vital that the younger generation of Chinese, who have only lived during a period of peace and growth in China and have no experience of China's tumultuous past, are made aware of the mistakes China made as a result of hubris and excesses in ideology. They have to be imbued with the right values and attitudes to meet the future with humility and responsibility. The authors of China's doctrine of peaceful emergence are acutely conscious that as China resumes its recovery, it has the responsibility and self-interest to assure its neighbors, and the world at large, that its emergence is benign, not a threat, but a plus for the world, that it will try to avoid disruption and conflict. . . . China is aware of the problems its rapid growth will present to the rest of the world and wishes to work together with the international community to minimize the disturbance. It is to the good of China to study how to mitigate the adverse impacts of its growth.[34]

The ways in which Chinese superiority will be expressed will undoubtedly be quite different than in the earlier era. Take the current case of East Asia, where they have, obviously, established a dominant economic position in relations with their neighbors, and used that position including access to a market of 1.3 billion people and significant investments in other countries to their advantage. If states or enterprises do not accept China's position and pay appropriate deference, they are faced with the threat of being shut out of a rapidly growing market with 1.3 billion people.[35]

CHAPTER 4

⊕

The Future of India

Will India rise to become a great power, and if so, on what timeline? What constraints does India's system of democratic governance impose on its long-term prospects? What constraints does India's culture impose on its long-term prospects? What are India's current economic strengths? What are India's long-term economic challenges and likely performance? What are India's economic prospects relative to China's in the next decade? How significant for the rest of Asia is India's democratic model, especially in contrast to China's authoritarian model? Can India serve in Asia as a strategic counterweight to China? What is the forecast for U.S.-India relations? As a long-time observer of India's economy, politics, and regional role, Lee Kuan Yew is uniquely positioned to answer the preceding questions.

✤

Will India rise to become a great power, and if so, on what timeline?

On my earlier visits in 1959 and 1962, when Nehru was in charge, I thought India showed promise of becoming a thriving society and a great power. By the late 1970s, I thought it would become a big military power . . . but not an economically thriving one because of its stifling bureaucracy.[1]

What constraints does India's system of democratic governance impose on its long-term prospects?

India has wasted decades in state planning and controls that have bogged it down in bureaucracy and corruption. A decentralized system would have allowed more centers like Bangalore and Bombay to grow and prosper. . . . The caste system has been the enemy of meritocracy. . . . India is a nation of unfulfilled greatness. Its potential has lain fallow, underused.[2]

There are limitations in the Indian constitutional system and the Indian political system that prevent it from going at high speed. . . . Whatever the political leadership may want to do, it must go through a very complex system at the center, and then even a more complex system in the various states. . . . Indians will go at a tempo which is decided by their constitution, by their ethnic mix, by their voting patterns, and the resulting coalition governments, which makes for very difficult decision-making.[3]

It is part of the constitutional system which has been accepted by the people and is established now. There will be a constant tinkering around with state boundaries, linguistic affinities, caste quotas. . . . All those adjustments detract from a dynamic meritocracy and prevent India from maximizing its potential.[4]

India's political leaders are determined to reform, but the Indian bureaucracy has been slower and resistant to change. Regional jostling and corruption do not help. Furthermore, populist democracy makes Indian policies less consistent, with regular changes in ruling parties. . . . India has poor infrastructure, high administrative and regulatory barriers to business, and large fiscal deficits, especially at the state level, that are a drag on investment and job creation.[5]

If all Indian ministers and top bureaucrats were like Narayana Murthy [cofounder and former chief executive officer of Infosys]— hardworking, tough taskmasters, hard negotiators, but always forward-looking—India would be one of the fastest-growing countries in the world, and in one generation would become a first-world country. However, Murthy probably realizes that no single person can change India's system of governance to become as efficient as Infosys.[6]

What constraints does India's culture impose on its long-term prospects?

India is not a real country. Instead, it is 32 separate nations that happen to be arrayed along the British rail line. The British came, conquered, established the Raj, incorporated under their rule an amalgam of 175 princely states, and ruled them with 1,000 Englishmen and several tens of thousands of Indians brought up to behave like English.[7]

I am against a society which has no sense of nurturing its best to rise to the top. I am against a feudal society where your birth decides where you stay in the pecking order. The example of that, par excellence, is India's caste system.[8]

India is an established civilization. Nehru and Gandhi had a chance to do for India what I did for Singapore because of their enormous prestige, but they could not break the caste system. They could not break the habits.[9]

Look at the construction industries in India and China, and you will know the difference between one that gets things done and another that does not get things done, but talks about things. . . . It is partly because India is such a diverse country—it is not one nation, but 32 different nations speaking 330 different dialects. . . . In China, it is 90% Han Chinese all speaking the same language, with different accents, but reading the same script. If you stand up in Delhi and speak in English, out of 1.2 billion people, maybe 200 million will understand you. If you speak in Hindi, maybe 250 million will understand you. If you speak in Tamil, 80 million people will understand you. So there is an enormous difference between the two countries. . . . We are comparing oranges and apples. . . . Let me not be misunderstood. The upper class in India is equal to any in the world. The Brahmins, who are the children of the priests . . .

are as bright and as smart as you can find anywhere in the world, but . . . they face the same hurdles. And also because, in their caste system, if you are a Brahmin and you marry a non-Brahmin, you go down in caste, so your genetic pool is frozen in each caste.[10]

The average Indian civil servant still sees himself primarily as a regulator and not as a facilitator. The average Indian bureaucrat has not yet accepted that it is not a sin to make profits and become rich. The average Indian bureaucrat has little trust in India's business community. They view Indian businesspeople as money-grabbing opportunists who do not have the welfare of the country at heart, and all the more so if they are foreign.[11]

What are India's current economic strengths?

India's private sector is superior to China's. . . . Indian companies follow international rules of corporate governance and offer a higher return on equity as against Chinese companies. And India has transparent and functioning capital markets.[12]

India has a stronger banking system and capital markets than China. India has stronger institutions—in particular, a well-developed legal system which should provide a better environment for the creation and protection of intellectual property.[13]

India—with an average age of 26, compared to China's 33, and with much faster population growth—will enjoy a bigger demographic dividend, but it will have to educate its people better, or else, the opportunity will turn into a burden.[14]

What are India's long-term economic challenges and likely performance?

Unless India moves away from its mindset, it will be a case of lost opportunities. . . . It has to build super highways, introduce super fast trains, and build bigger and better airports. It will also have to accept that to be a developed nation, it has to move its people from the villages to urban areas, as China is doing.[15]

After Indira Gandhi's son died, I said to her . . . "Take this chance, open up India, change the policy. Look at Indians overseas, see how well they are doing in England, in Singapore, all over the world. You are confining and conscribing them by your policies, by your bureaucracy." She told me: "I cannot do it. This is this. That is the way India is". . . . I did not see anybody else. She had the gumption to declare a state of emergency, and by the time you have the guts to do that, you should have the guts to change the system and let Indian enterprise break out. So that was when I became resigned that India was going to go the slow path. And at that time, I saw China rising . . . breaking away from communism. So I knew that the race would not be an equal one. I gave up.[16]

India is a thicket of rules and regulations and bureaucracy that you have to find your way through.[17]

India probably has three to five years to fix its infrastructure. If it does not, it risks losing out in the global economic sweepstakes.[18]

India must emulate the effective way in which China has built up its extensive communications and transportation infrastructure, power plants, and water resources, and implements policies that lead to huge FDIs [foreign direct investments] in manufacturing, high job creation, and high growth. India's spectacular growth has been in IT [information technology] services, which do not generate high job creation.[19]

The moment India has the infrastructure in place, investments will come in, and it will catch up very fast. What India needs is a more liberalized system which allows more international competition to enter. Then it will be able to play to the level of international companies.[20]

India lacks fast connectivity between cities. . . . Once it gets its logistics right—roads, ports, railways—and cuts down red tape, it will get jobs not only in IT, but in manufacturing and all. Jobs will grow, and the country will be transformed.[21]

To create jobs, the main thrust of reforms must be in manufacturing. That requires a change in labor laws to allow employers to retrench workers when business demand is down, streamlining the judicial processes, reducing the fiscal deficit, loosening up the bureaucracy, and most of all, improving infrastructure.[22]

India cannot grow into a major economy on services alone. Since the industrial revolution, no country has become a major economy without becoming an industrial power.[23]

Corruption bedevils both, but bureaucratic red tape has lowered India's efficiency and effectiveness more than China's.[24]

India needs to, first of all, cut down on red tapeism; second, provide greater incentives for the private sector; third, address the challenge of infrastructure shortages; and, finally, liberalize foreign direct investment norms in the country.[25]

Even now when India liberalizes, it sells state-owned enterprises but says that it cannot dismiss workers. How the hell is it going to make them profitable? How can it expand and make them productive and begin to employ workers on a different basis?[26]

India's narrower band of educated people will be a weakness in the longer term. And although top-quality Indian manpower is in high demand, large numbers of engineers and graduates lack the skills required in a changing economy and remain unemployed. . . . Only over half of each Indian cohort completes primary school, a big loss.[27]

India's leaders, starting with Nehru and his generation, were mesmerized by the supposedly rapid growth and industrialization of the Soviet Union. And, of course, this is what British economists of the time . . . were recommending: big capital accumulation, big projects, iron, steel, making agricultural implements. Then you develop. . . . They believed in it. . . . When India started changing in 1991, '92 with Manmohan Singh, who was himself a planner, they had already lost 40 years of growth. They had the problem now of dismantling all these monopolies. And the unions are now part and parcel of these big state-owned companies, who do not want them to be privatized, because if you run them efficiently, the workforce will be reduced by two-thirds or one-half.[28]

India's history has left it skeptical of foreign investments and inward-looking in economics. . . . Policies of self-reliance are no longer relevant in an interdependent world with fast-changing technology. . . . A second relic of India's historical legacy is its preoccupation with fair distribution. . . . To redistribute all the gains in the early stages of growth will slow down the capital accumulation necessary to generate further growth. Wealth springs from entrepreneurship, which means risk taking. . . . The only way to raise the living conditions of the poor is to increase the size of the pie. Equality of incomes gives no incentive to the resourceful and the industrious to outperform and be competitive.[29]

The lack of an economically educated electorate has made it easy for India's leaders to engage in economic populism, which has unsettled the course of liberalization. National interest is often subservient to special interests. Many needed reforms have been stalled due to opposition from special interest groups. Special interests thrive in an atmosphere of populism. In the last 20 years, there has been a proliferation of schemes for cheap food, free power, and subsidized loans. . . . They impose a heavy cost on the whole economy. . . . The distinction between welfare and populism has blurred.[30]

There are three Indian schools in Singapore. There were going to be more, but I said no. You either go to a Singapore school or you go back to India, because . . . even if they [Indians] stay on as permanent residents and do national service, they are not readily absorbed because they have been oriented toward Indian culture. . . . The textbooks in these schools are all India-oriented, the knowledge is Indian, the sentiments, and everything. That is the problem.[31]

India had many first-rate universities at independence. Except for a few top universities such as the Indian Institutes of Technology and Indian Institutes of Management that still rank with the best, it could not maintain the high standards of its many other universities. Political pressures made for quotas for admission based on caste or connections with members of parliament.[32]

What are India's economic prospects relative to China's in the next decade?

Do not talk about India and China in the same breath. They are two different countries. But does that make India a non-player? No. It is a bigger player than the whole of ASEAN [the Association of Southeast Asian Nations] put together.[33]

The systems are not comparable. . . . China's GDP [gross domestic product] is three and a half times that of India. India is growing at about two-thirds the rate of China. But India is a big country and a counterweight in the Indian Ocean.[34]

India's economy can grow to about 60–70% that of China. . . . It is not going to be bigger—on present projections. But 60–70% of China with a population which will be bigger than China's by 2050 is something considerable, and India has some very able people at the top.[35]

Why has China's peaceful rise, however, raised apprehensions? Is it because India is a democracy in which numerous political forces are constantly at work, making for an internal system of checks and balances? Most probably, yes—especially as India's governments have tended to be made up of large coalitions of 10 to 20 parties. . . . . India can project power across its borders farther and better than China can, yet there is no fear that India has aggressive intentions. . . . . India does not pose such a challenge to international order as China—and will not until it gets its social infrastructure up to First World standards and further liberalizes its economy. Indeed, the U.S., the European Union, and Japan root for India because they want a better-balanced world, in which India approximates China's weight. . . . . What if India were well ahead of China? Would Americans and Europeans be rooting for China? I doubt it. They still have a phobia of the "yellow peril," one reinforced by memories of the outrages of the Cultural Revolution and the massacres in Tiananmen Square, not to mention their strong feelings against Chinese government censorship.[36]

China is focused on the U.S. and just wants to keep the Indians at arm's length.[37]

I am not sure that India wants a piece of the consumer demand from China's growing middle class, because India is scared of the competition. The Chinese have offered the Indians a free-trade agreement, but the Indians have not snapped at it because Chinese goods will go into India and compete.[38]

As long as there is free-market bargaining, India will just have to learn to outbid China. China will not go to war with India. It is prepared to take risks; for example, it is in the Niger Delta, risking

Chinese lives with Chinese money, but it has decided that it is worth it. It is in Angola and Sudan. It wants something out of Iran. It is making friends with the Central Asian republics. It wants a pipeline from Kazakhstan into China over thousands of kilometers, and it is prepared to build it. This is free-market competition. I do not see it as being, "If you agree to sell to India, I will beat you up," but rather as, "Whatever India offers you, I will offer you more." It is going to play by the rules of the game and is quite convinced that it can win that way.[39]

How significant for the rest of Asia is India's democratic model, especially in contrast to China's authoritarian model?

It would be significant if it was achieving better results than China's model, but it is not.[40]

Political systems that yield inferior economic performance will ultimately be discarded for those that are more productive.[41]

Democracy should not be made an alibi for inertia. There are many examples of authoritarian governments whose economies have failed. There are as many examples of democratic governments who have achieved superior economic performance. The real issue is whether any country's political system, irrespective of whether it is democratic or authoritarian, can forge a consensus on the policies needed for the economy to grow and create jobs for all, and can ensure that these basic policies are implemented consistently without large leakage.[42]

India's system of democracy and rule of law gives it a long-term advantage over China, although in the early phases, China has the advantage of faster implementation of its reforms.[43]

If China's political structures do not adjust to accommodate the changes in its society resulting from high rates of growth, India will have an advantage because of its more flexible political system in the longer term.[44]

Can India serve in Asia as a strategic counterweight to China?

I have a selfish motive in wanting India to emerge as early as possible as a major economic power in world politics. If India does not emerge, Asia will be submerged (Lee's statement to J. R. D. Tata in 1974).[45]

"Lee Kuan Yew emphasized the necessity of an Indian presence in the region, either through a multilateral security arrangement or by the enunciation of an 'Asian Monroe Doctrine' to dissuade possible 'poaching' in Asia. He said India was the ideal candidate to undertake such a role because she had been conducting her foreign policy 'on a basis of equality and not on a basis of power relations.' The role that he envisaged for India was that of a 'guardian' as he urged 'India to take an active interest in the security, political stability, and economic development of the smaller

Southeast Asian nations'" (Sunanda K. Datta-Ray's assessment of Lee's view of Southeast Asia following the withdrawal of Western powers in the late 1970s).[46]

Korea is too small. Vietnam is too small. Southeast Asia is too disparate. You need another big player to hold the balance.[47]

Who is the counterweight? Japan cannot be the counterweight. . . . Together, Japan and America can be a counterweight, economically, physically, and militarily, but who is the X counterweight within Asia, because America may, in 100 or 200 years, become less able to dominate Asia? But the Indians are here for keeps.[48]

India has succeeded in modernizing its armed forces, especially its navy, and defending its security. Although the Chinese are building a port in Burma and another in Pakistan, India will dominate the Indian Ocean for a long time.[49]

India does not geographically fit in the Pacific. But the contest between the U.S. and China will be in the Pacific and the Indian Ocean. China has moved naval forces into the Indian Ocean to protect its oil supply from the Gulf, and commodities from Africa. That is where the Indians are a force. If the Indians are on the American side, the Americans will have a great advantage. So the Chinese have to have a counter, and have developed ports in Myanmar and in Pakistan.[50]

India does not exert much economic or geopolitical influence in Southeast Asia because the region's attention is focused on China, which is the source of power projection.[51]

What is the forecast for U.S.-India relations?

There is no immediate U.S.-India strategic partnership to encircle China. Even when the relationship grows, India will remain an independent player. It will defend its interests with China and cooperate with China where their interests coincide.[52]

CHAPTER 5

＋

The Future of Islamic Extremism

What threat does Islamic extremism pose to the West? What are the roots of Islamic extremism? What role does Islam itself play in fueling Islamic extremism? What are the key objectives of Islamic extremists? How likely are Islamic extremists to achieve those objectives? What factors will affect the future of Islamic extremism? What role do moderate Muslims play in fighting Islamic extremism? How long will Islamic extremism pose a threat to global security? Lee Kuan Yew's answers to these questions reflect the fact that Singapore's neighbors are Muslim countries and that Singapore has been a potential target of terrorist attacks.

⊕

What threat does Islamic extremism pose to the West?

The big divide is no longer between communist and democratic countries, or between West and East. Now it is between Muslim terrorists and the U.S., Israel, and their supporters. A secondary battle is between militant Islam and non-militant modernist Islam.[1]

We are faced with a new situation, never faced before in the history of civilization. We have a group of people willing to destroy themselves to inflict damage on others. The only ones before them were the Tamil Tigers. But they were fighting for a tangible cause, for a homeland for Tamils in Sri Lanka. This is fighting for Islam, a different cause springing from a religious conviction.[2]

Al Qaeda-style terrorism is new and unique because it is global. An event in Morocco can excite the passions of extremist groups in Indonesia. There is a shared fanatical zealousness among these different extremists around the world.[3]

This surge in Islamist terrorism will take years to tamp down. In the meantime, the world is at risk of these terrorists acquiring weapons of mass destruction. Were that to happen, the slaughter would be horrendous. The nuclear programs of rogue states, therefore, must be stopped, and their stockpiles of weapons and material confiscated.[4]

Islam has not been a problem. However, contemporary radical Islam, or Islamism, is a problem. Oil without Islamism can be a problem, but Islamism *plus* oil becomes a volatile mix. Islamism *plus* oil *plus* weapons of mass destruction equals a threat. . . . A nuclear-capable Iran will significantly alter the geopolitical balance. Other countries in the Middle East will also want nuclear weapons, increasing the chances that fissile material for WMD [weapons of mass destruction] will fall into terrorists' hands.[5]

What are the roots of Islamic extremism?

The Israeli-Palestinian conflict is not the cause of Islamic terrorism. Among Muslims, especially in the Middle East, there is a profound belief that their time has come and that the West has put them down for too long. While pan-Arab nationalism failed to unite the Muslim world in the 1950s and 1960s, Islamic fervor has become an alternative unifying force.[6]

Militant Islam feeds upon the insecurities and alienation that globalization generates among the less successful. And because globalization is largely U.S.-led and driven, militant Islam identifies America and Americans as the threat to Islam. That America steadfastly supports Israel aggravates their sense of threat. But terrorism would continue even if the Middle East problem were solved.[7]

Ever since the founding of Israel, Arabs in the Middle East have been taught to hate Israelis and Jews in their schools, madrassas, and mosques, reinforced regularly by repeated media images of powerful Israeli military incursions into the occupied Palestinian territories. After 40 years of patchy economic development, many Arabs feel anger and humiliation that their once glorious Islamic civilization has been diminished by the West, especially America, and corrupted by its licentious culture. . . . Ending the Palestinian conflict will deprive extremists of a convenient rallying point. But unless militant groups in the Arab countries and Islamic theocracies are seen to fail, Jemaah Islamiyah and other militant groups in the non-Arab Muslim world will continue to recruit extremists. Even if there is an Israeli-Palestinian settlement, the U.S. and its Western allies must ensure that Islamic militancy is defeated by economic, military, and other means to clearly demonstrate to non-Arab Muslims that fanaticism and militancy have no future.[8]

The nature of Islam in Southeast Asia has been changing over the last 30 years. First and foremost, after the price of oil quadrupled in 1973, Saudi Arabia has generously financed the missionary movement by building mosques and religious schools and paying for preachers throughout the world, spreading the teachings and practices of its austere version of Wahhabist Islam. Next, the overthrow of the Shah in Iran in 1979 . . . has had a profound impact on Muslim beliefs in Islam's power. Finally, the participation of large numbers of Southeast Asian Muslims in the jihad in Afghanistan during the 1980s and the 1990s has radicalized significant numbers of the Southeast Asian Muslims.[9]

When we asked our Muslims, "Why have you become so strict in your religious practices?" they answered, "Because we are better educated and so understand better what must be observed." But the bigger factor is the peer pressure from the heart of the Muslim world. With the increase in religiosity worldwide as a result of Saudi funding of mosques, madrassas, and religious teachers, whole populations are geared up. Then some of those in a high pitch are hijacked by the extremist radicals to become jihadists. Al Qaeda and their local extremists recruit from the mosques those who look suitable for their own private religious classes, where they are taught that it is the duty of all good Muslims to fight for all oppressed Muslims worldwide, and, if necessary, to die for the cause, to become martyrs.[10]

In Southeast Asia, the Muslims are different. They are relaxed, easy to get on with. But over the last 30-odd years, since the oil crisis and the petrodollars became a major factor in the Muslim world, the extremists have been proselytizing, building mosques, religious schools where they teach Wahhabism . . . sending out preachers, and having conferences. Globalizing, networking. And slowly they have convinced the Southeast Asian Muslims, and indeed Muslims throughout the world, that the gold standard is Saudi Arabia, that that is the real good Muslim.[11]

What role does Islam itself play in fueling Islamic extremism?

Muslims want to assimilate us. It is one-way traffic. . . . They have no confidence in allowing choice.[12]

Samuel Huntington sent me a piece he was writing in *Foreign Affairs* called the "Clash of Civilizations." When I saw him, I said, look, I agree with you only where the Muslims are concerned, only there. . . . Hinduism, Chinese Confucianism or Communism, Japanese Shintoism, they are secular really. They know that to progress, you must master science and technology. . . . But the Muslims believe that if they master the Qu'ran and they are prepared to do all that Muhammad has prescribed, they will succeed. So, we can expect trouble from them and so, it happened.[13]

Muslims socially do not cause any trouble, but they are distinct and separate. . . . Islam is exclusive.[14]

What are the key objectives of Islamic extremists?

Islamists believe the time is ripe to reassert Islam's supremacy. The jihadists among them have chosen Iraq as their second battleground. Their goal is to drive the Americans out of Iraq, just as they drove the Soviets out of Afghanistan. . . . Radical Islamic groups in several countries want to engineer a clash of civilizations, and oil power has given them the means.[15]

What Osama bin Laden wants is to get all of the oil of the Gulf states and institute Taliban-type regimes. Then he will have all the industrialized countries—Christian Europe, America, Japan, China—by the throat. Then they will be able to have their Muslim caliphate across the world.[16]

Has the situation in Iraq made terrorism worse? In the short term, yes. But terrorism was already set to get worse. Before the war in Iraq, jihadist acolytes in Singapore, Indonesia, the Philippines,

Spain, Holland, England, and many other countries were being prepared for martyrdom by their imams. The jihadists want to destroy Israel and drive the U.S. out of the oil states of the Gulf. This witch's brew of hate would have been on the boil regardless of U.S. actions in Iraq or Afghanistan. The random killing will go on for years and will stop only when the jihadists and their teachers realize that instead of bending it to their will, the bombing of innocent people has turned the world—including many Muslim countries, such as Jordan—against them.[17]

How likely are Islamic extremists to achieve those objectives?

The Al Qaeda Islamic extremists believe that by repeated huge suicide bombings, they can drive the Americans out of the Middle East, destroy America, and frighten Europe, and thereby keep their Muslim societies pure and pious, as in the seventh century. They cannot succeed, because technology will continue to develop and change our economies and our lifestyles, whether we are Christians, Muslims, Jews, Buddhists, Hindus, atheists, or agnostics.[18]

I do not see the Islamic extremists winning, and by that I mean able to impose their extremist system. I can see them inducing fear and insecurity, and causing fear, but they do not have the technology and the organization to overwhelm any government.[19]

They want to create . . . a caliphate that comprises Malaysia, Indonesia, the southern Philippines, and Singapore. It is absurd, not achievable. . . . Why should Thai, Malaysian, or Filipino

Muslims give up power and surrender sovereignty to this caliphate led by Indonesians? . . . It may take another 20, 30 years . . . but the theocratic state will fail. And successive failures in the Muslim world will show that the theocratic state, like the communist state, is a mirage.[20]

Islamic terrorists will gradually lose their capacity to strike such fear in Europe and the U.S., as these countries take stiff and comprehensive measures to counter them. . . . If Muslims in Europe and the U.S. do not distance themselves and expose these terrorists in their midst, they will be feared and ostracized. They will find it difficult to get good jobs. In Muslim countries, it is a matter of time before the moderate Muslims have to put down the extremists, or they will end up with Taliban governments in charge of them, as in Afghanistan.[21]

With the killing of Osama bin Laden, the Islamic extremist movement has been franchised out, and each group works on its own. It is accordingly more diverse and difficult to pin down. At the same time, however, splinter terrorist groups do not have the intellectual capacity to imagine and execute attacks on the scale of 9/11.[22]

What factors will affect the future of Islamic extremism?

Whether Islamic extremism is a bigger or smaller problem 10, 15, or 25 years from now depends on what happens in the oil states, particularly Saudi Arabia.[23]

The costs of leaving Iraq unstable would be high. Jihadists everywhere would be emboldened. . . . A few years ago, the Taliban in Afghanistan and Saddam Hussein's Iraq were a check on Iran. The Taliban is again gathering strength, and a Taliban victory in Afghanistan or Pakistan would reverberate throughout the Muslim world. It would influence the grand debate among Muslims on the future of Islam. A severely retrograde form of Islam would be seen to have defeated modernity twice: first the Soviet Union, then the United States. There would be profound consequences, especially in the campaign against terrorism.[24]

If the United States leaves Iraq prematurely, jihadists everywhere will be emboldened to take the battle to Washington and its friends and allies. Having defeated the Russians in Afghanistan and the United States in Iraq, they will believe that they can change the world. Even worse, if civil war breaks out in Iraq, the conflict will destabilize the whole Middle East, as it will draw in Egypt, Iran, Jordan, Lebanon, Saudi Arabia, Syria, and Turkey.[25]

If U.S. forces leave Iraq precipitately because of terrorist attacks, Muslim terrorists throughout the world will be triumphant. Where the Vietnamese were content to see Americans leave and to concentrate on building socialism in Vietnam, Islamic militants will pursue departing Americans to all corners of the globe. If the militants succeed in thwarting the U.S. in Iraq, their zealousness to die in pursuit of an Islamic caliphate spanning the globe will reach new heights.[26]

What role do moderate Muslims play in fighting Islamic extremism?

Only Muslims can win this struggle. Moderate, modernizing Muslims, political, religious, civic leaders together have to make the case against the fundamentalists. But the strong, developed countries can help. The NATO [North Atlantic Treaty Organization] allies must . . . present a solid block. Muslim modernizers must feel that the U.S. and its allies will provide the resources, energy, and support to make them winners. No one wants to be on the losing side.[27]

Only Muslims themselves—those with a moderate, more modern approach to life—can fight the fundamentalists for control of the Muslim soul. Muslims must counter the terrorist ideology that is based on a perverted interpretation of Islam. This battle will be joined when the fundamentalist Islamic terrorists seek to displace their present Muslim leaders, as they must if they are to set up their version of the Islamic state.[28]

I did talk about extremist terrorists like the Jemaah Islamiyah group, and the jihadist preachers who brainwashed them. They are implacable in wanting to put down all who do not agree with them. So their Islam is a perverted version, which the overwhelming majority of Muslims in Singapore do not subscribe to. I also pointed out that our Muslim leaders are rational, and that the ultimate solution to extremist terrorism was to give moderate Muslims the courage to stand up and speak out against radicals who have hijacked Islam to recruit volunteers for their violent ends.[29]

At first sight, this is a struggle between extremist radicals in the Muslim world on one side and America, Israel, and their Western allies on the other. But look deeper and you will see that at its heart, it is a struggle about what Islam means between the extremist Muslims and the rationalist Muslims, between fundamentalist Muslims and modernist Muslims.[30]

Eventually, the fight will boil down to one between Muslims who want to return to the Islam of the 11th century (when Islam shut out the outside world and cut itself off from new ideas) and those who want to see a modern Islam attuned to the 21st century. If the West were to reach a consensus and agree on their strategy against terrorists, as it did during the Cold War, then together with Japan, China, and Russia, moderate Muslims who want to modernize their societies would have confidence and courage to take on the extremists and stop them from producing more terrorists.[31]

Moderates in the Muslim world, by not being able to take a stand and take the lead and start the argument with the extremists in the mosques, in the madrassas, they are ducking the issue and allowing the extremists to hijack not just Islam, but the whole of the Muslim community.[32]

The majority of Muslims have nothing to do with terrorism or extremism. However, militant terrorist groups have hijacked Islam as their driving force and have given it a virulent twist. Throughout the Muslim world, the militants are out to impose their version of Islam. The majority of Muslims who are moderates are caught in between (1) their sympathy for and identification with the Palestinians and anger against the Israelis, and (2) their desire for a peaceful life of growth and progress. To resolve the problem of terrorism, the U.S. and others must support the tolerant non-militant Muslims so that they will prevail.[33]

To stop the increase in terrorist recruits, the U.S. and Europe must discredit extremist ideology, which takes Qu'ranic passages out of context, preaches hatred against non-Muslims, and seeks to spread Islam through violence. Muslims who want to be a part of the modern world of science and technology must confront and stop these Islamists from preaching violence and hatred. They must get the Muslim scholars and religious teachers to preach that Islam is a religion of peace, not terror, and that it is tolerant of other peoples and their faiths. . . . In countries where Muslims are a minority, as in Britain, they must take a clear-cut stand against Islamist terrorists. . . . In Muslim countries such as Pakistan and Iraq, Muslims will be forced to confront the Islamists or witness their governments being overthrown and their people dragged back into a feudal past, just as the Taliban did in Afghanistan.[34]

The United States must be more multilateral in its approach to isolating jihadist groups and rally Europe, Russia, China, India, and all non-Muslim governments to its cause, along with many moderate Muslims. A worldwide coalition is necessary to fight the fires of hatred that the Islamist fanatics are fanning. When moderate Muslim governments, such as those in Indonesia, Malaysia, the Persian Gulf states, Egypt, and Jordan, feel comfortable associating themselves openly with a multilateral coalition against Islamist terrorism, the tide of battle will turn against the extremists.[35]

To make the long-term burden sustainable, the U.S. needs a broad alliance, to spread the load, to reduce excessive burdens on itself. It needs others to agree on the basic causes and solutions. It is not poverty, it is not deprivation, it is something more fundamental, a resurgence of Arab and Islamic pride, and a belief that their time has come. The objective must be to reassure and persuade moderate Muslims . . . that they are not going to lose, that they have the weight, the resources of the world behind them. They must have the courage to go into the mosques and madrassas and switch off the radicals.[36]

How long will Islamic extremism pose a threat to global security?

Islamic terrorism has been brewing since the 1970s and cannot be taken off the boil easily or soon. The war against terrorism will be long and arduous. Terrorists, the existence of weapons of mass destruction, and the continuing Israeli-Palestinian conflict will be threats for many years.[37]

Islamic terrorism is going to be a problem for this world for a very long time, and that problem will not change whoever wins the 2004 U.S. presidential elections.[38]

The problem of Islamic terrorism will not be easily extirpated. . . . Moderate Muslims have to be encouraged to stand up and speak out against radicalism. They need confidence that they can. We can get to the tipping point, but I do not know how long it will take. . . . Islamic terrorists will continue to use violence until shown that their methods will not succeed. If they are successful in Iraq, they will try to topple secular governments in other countries, such as Indonesia.[39]

Americans make the mistake of seeking largely a military solution. You must use force. But force will only deal with the tip of the problem. In killing the terrorists, you will only kill the worker bees. The queen bees are the preachers, who teach a deviant form of Islam in schools and Islamic centers, who capture and twist the minds of the young. . . . Terrorists say: "I will be happy to die a martyr. After me there will be a million others."[40]

We should learn to live with the Pakistan-terror nexus for a long time. My fear is Pakistan may well get worse.[41]

CHAPTER 6

The Future of National Economic Growth

hat are the lessons of Singapore's rise from the third world to the first world in one generation? What are the chief drivers of national growth and competitiveness? What role do more intangible factors such as values play in driving growth and competitiveness? What core competencies should today's worker possess? Lee Kuan Yew's insightful answers to these questions draw on his remarkable experience in taking Singapore from the third world to the first world in a few decades.

What are the lessons of Singapore's rise from the third world to the first world in one generation?

My definition of a Singaporean . . . is that we accept that whoever joins us is part of us. And that is an American concept. You can keep your name, Brzezinski, Berlusconi, whatever it is, you have come, join me, you are American. We need talent, we accept them. That must be our defining attribute.[1]

When I started, the question was how Singapore can make a living against neighbors who have more natural resources, human resources, and bigger space. How did we differentiate ourselves from them? They are not clean systems; we run clean systems. Their rule of law is wonky; we stick to the law. Once we come to an agreement or make a decision, we stick to it. We become reliable and credible to investors. World-class infrastructure, world-class supporting staff, all educated in English. Good communications by air, by sea, by cable, by satellite, and now, over the Internet.[2]

Make haste slowly. Nobody likes to lose his ethnic, cultural, religious, even linguistic identity. To exist as one state, you need to share certain attributes, have things in common. If you pressure-cook, you are in for problems. If you go gently, but steadily, the logic of events will bring about not assimilation, but integration. If I had tried to foist the English language on the people of Singapore, I would have faced rebellion all around. If I had tried to foist the Chinese language, I would have had immediate revolt and disaster.

But I offered every parent a choice of English and their mother tongue, in whatever order they chose. By their free choice, plus the rewards of the marketplace over a period of 30 years, we have ended up with English first and the mother tongue second. We have switched one university already established in the Chinese language from Chinese into English. Had this change been forced in five or ten years instead of being done over 30 years—and by free choice—it would have been a disaster.[3]

Most failures in the third world were the result of the leaders of the immediate post-independence period, the 1960s to the 1980s, abiding by the theory then prevailing that socialism and state enterprises would hasten development. Their interventionist economic policies led to misallocation of resources and increased opportunities for corruption. That theory was demolished as a result of the collapse of the Soviet Union. There is no reason why third world leaders cannot succeed in achieving growth and development if they can maintain social order, educate their people, maintain peace with their neighbors, and gain the confidence of investors by upholding the rule of law.[4]

What are the chief drivers of national growth and competitiveness?

A people's standard of living depends on a number of basic factors: first, the resources it has in relation to its population . . . ; second, its level of technological competence and standards of industrial development; third, its educational and training standards; and fourth, the culture, the discipline, and drive in the workforce.[5]

Demography, not democracy, will be the most critical factor for security and growth in the 21st century. . . . Countries that most welcome migrants have an economic advantage, but open immigration policies also carry risks. New waves of migrants will be ethnically different, less educated, and sometimes unskilled. . . . It will gradually dawn on governments that immigration alone cannot solve their demographic troubles and that much more active government involvement in encouraging or discouraging procreation may be necessary.[6]

The quality of a nation's manpower resources is the single most important factor determining national competitiveness. It is a people's innovativeness, entrepreneurship, team work, and their work ethic that give them that sharp keen edge in competitiveness.[7]

Three attributes are vital in this competition—entrepreneurship, innovation, and management. The first is the entrepreneurship to seek out new opportunities and to take calculated risks. Standing still is a sure way to extinction. . . . The second attribute, innovation, is what creates new products and processes that add value. . . . The third factor is good management. To grow, company managements have to open up new markets and create new distribution channels.[8]

The economy is driven by new knowledge, new discoveries in science and technology, innovations that are taken to the market by entrepreneurs. So while the scholar is still the greatest factor in economic progress, he will be so only if he uses his brains—not in studying the great books, classical texts, and poetry, but in capturing and discovering new knowledge, applying himself in research and development, management and marketing, banking and finance, and the myriad of new subjects that need to be mastered. Those with good minds to be scholars should also become inventors, innovators, venture capitalists, and entrepreneurs; they must bring new products and services to the market to enrich the lives of people everywhere.[9]

The global landscape for investments is changing. First, advances in technology and globalization have reduced the cost of outsourcing, made distance less of a barrier, and changed the economics of how businesses can best structure their operations across countries. . . . Second, technology and innovation have become more important factors for economic success. The 2000 World Economic Forum Competitiveness ranking placed increased emphasis on economic creativity. The report distinguished between innovative countries and countries that are merely good recipients of technology transfer, reflecting the weight investors give to technological sophistication, and not simply low wage costs. Third, competition for investment has intensified. . . . The key to innovation and technology is people. We must develop and nurture our talent so that innovation and creativity will be integral to education and training. Our education system is being revamped to nurture innovation and creativity, from kindergarten to university, and on to lifelong learning.[10]

There is now a global marketplace as goods, services, capital, and knowledge become even more mobile. These developments have accelerated the integration of regional markets. However, in order to benefit from globalization, countries must ensure that their laws and institutions facilitate the global flow. There is a fundamental need for the rule of law. It ensures stability and predictability. Next, between participating countries, a congruence of laws and rules governing trade and investment will develop. It eases economic activity by lowering transaction costs. The Roman and British Empires were examples in history of how trade flourished for hundreds of years under the protection of a comprehensive, unified system of laws.[11]

Businesses now source for talent and opportunities globally. They invent, collaborate, or acquire technologies and capabilities globally to ensure their competitive edge. As the Internet makes more markets contestable, businesses in Asia must compete on this platform or be swept aside. The national counterpart to businesses that source globally is a society that welcomes foreign talent. Societies that will succeed are those which easily assimilate foreigners. Silicon Valley is such a place. Not only is it "color blind" and uniquely meritocratic, it has a culture that draws newcomers in. Asia's businesspeople must acquire these attributes and be globally literate.[12]

Convergence and competition will also bring about changes at the firm and industry level. Multinational corporations will become multicultural organizations in order to compete successfully in knowledge-based sectors. Corporations that get their ideas from only one culture will lose out in innovation. Those that have a creative meshing of cultures and ideas will forge ahead. . . . To be competitive globally, firms will have to employ talents for key positions from the countries they operate in. Corporations will need the best people from throughout the world for key positions. . . . Management guru Peter Drucker has predicted that the greatest change in the way business is to be conducted in the next century will be the accelerating growth of relationships based not on ownership but on *partnership.*[13]

We must continue to attract as many able and talented people from China, India, the region, and from developed countries, to add to our team. Without this input of foreign talent, even the U.S. could not have been so successful. Their atomic bomb owed much to European talent fleeing from Hitler in the 1930s and 40s. . . . Even the American space program owed its start to the German rocket scientist [Wernher] von Braun, who invented the V bomb in WWII and was captured by the U.S. army as the war ended. He was taken to America. Since then, every year, thousands of talented professionals, academics, researchers, and writers are drawn from the UK and EU [European Union] to the U.S. because they are made welcome in America and given the facilities for their research or

become successful in their professions or business. This has en-
hanced America's high performance. If America, with 280 million
people, needs to top up with talent, Singapore, with 3 million, must
do so, or we will be relegated to the second or third division.[14]

We draw our talent from only 3 million people. A short mountain range is unlikely to have peaks that can equal Mount Everest.
You need a long mountain range like the Himalayas unless you are
a special people like the Jews in Israel. With a population of
four million Jews, they have the talents of a population of more than
40 million. Everyone knows that Shanghainese are the brightest
and sharpest of people. But few know why. It is because, for over
150 years, ever since it became a treaty port for the foreign powers, it has drawn the ambitious, energetic, and talented from
the Yangtze Delta, Zhejiang, Jiangsu, and other provinces along
the river, a catchment of some 200–300 million. Even though
Shanghai regularly loses leaders to Beijing, it still has an abundance of talent, because it does not depend only on the 12 million in
the city itself.[15]

The impressive advance of those industrial countries whose
workforces are productivity-conscious, like Japan, and the sad decline of those countries in Europe with workforces bogged down by
negative union attitudes, like Britain, hold obvious lessons from
which we must learn. Singaporeans must take to heart one simple
fact: unless we improve ourselves through education and training,

and through developing the will to be productive, our future cannot be assured.[16]

The pressure of envy is inevitable. But consider the alternative, which is slow growth. The disparity will still be there between the high end and the low end because of globalization, but we are all poorer, right? . . . I see no benefit in stopping growth, because the envy will still be there.[17]

What role do more intangible factors such as values play in driving growth and competitiveness?

Besides the standard economic yardsticks for productivity and competitiveness, there are intangible factors like culture, religion, and other ethnic characteristics and national ethos that affect the outcome. . . . For a modern economy to succeed, a whole population must be educated. . . . China has built much better physical infrastructure than India. . . . The Chinese bureaucracy has been methodical in adopting best practices in their system of governance and public policies. . . . All said and done, it is the creativity of the leadership, its willingness to learn from experience elsewhere, to implement good ideas quickly and decisively through an efficient public service, and to convince the majority of people that tough reforms are worth taking, that decide a country's development and progress.[18]

More important than technological capabilities is the spirit of innovation and enterprise. In an era of startling technological change, it is the enterprising individuals, prepared to seize new opportunities, the creators of new ideas and businesses, who forge ahead. Ordinary businesspeople can make a living by being good followers, but the rich rewards go to innovators and entrepreneurs.[19]

Where do you produce your entrepreneurs from? Out of a top hat? . . . There is a dearth of entrepreneurial talent in Singapore. . . . We have to start experimenting. The easy things—just getting a blank mind to take in knowledge and become trainable—we have done. Now comes the difficult part. To get literate and numerate minds to be more innovative, to be more productive, is not easy. It requires a mindset change, a different set of values.[20]

Habits that make for high productivity in workers are the result of the values implanted in them at home, in school, and at the workplace. These values must be reinforced by the attitudes of society. Once established, like a language a society speaks, the habits tend to become a self-reproducing, self-perpetuating cycle. . . . I am astonished to find . . . that 55% of our workers still admit to the fear of being disliked by fellow workers for doing their job well. As long as this attitude persists, higher performance will be discouraged by the prevailing standards of mediocre workers. Better workers will refrain from becoming pace-setters. This attitude is negative. Singaporeans must understand that their group interests will be advanced if each worker strives to achieve his best, and thus encourages his peers to do better, by his example. There is no better way than the personal example of managers and grassroots leaders to bring about this change of attitudes and values. Old-fashioned notions that managers are out to exploit workers are irrelevant in today's industrial climate. Equally outmoded also are management views that trade unionists are troublemakers. These are mindsets of the past. They are stereotypes to be banished if we are to build up relationships of confidence and cooperation between management, unionists, and workers.[21]

We have focused on basics in Singapore. We used the family to push economic growth, factoring the ambitions of a person and his family into our planning. We have tried, for example, to improve the lot of children through education. The government can create a setting in which people can live happily and succeed and express themselves, but finally it is what people do with their lives that determines economic success or failure. Again, we were fortunate we had this cultural backdrop, the belief in thrift, hard work, filial piety, and loyalty in the extended family, and, most of all, the respect for scholarship and learning. There is, of course, another reason for our success. We have been able to create economic growth because we facilitated certain changes while we moved from an agricultural society to an industrial society. We had the advantage of knowing what the end result should be by looking at the West and later Japan.[22]

Language and culture must both change to enable a people to solve new problems. Indeed the strength of the language and culture depends on their suppleness to help the people adjust to changed conditions. For example, Japanese language and culture of a century ago since the Meiji Restoration of 1868 have been considerably developed and adjusted to meet new needs. The Japanese people successfully adopted Western science and technology because they were supple and pragmatic about their language and culture. They borrowed new Western institutions and ideas. They introduced universal education, created a two-chamber parliament, introduced legal codes, and revamped their army and navy along German and British models. They freely adopted Western words, adding vigor to the Japanese language. Similarly, after defeat in World War II, during and after the American occupation of Japan, American words, ideas, and social organizations were adapted and adopted by control from the Americans and improved on them, just as they had copied and improved on many Chinese innovations like the abacus.[23]

What core competencies should today's worker possess?

Unlike workers in the repetitive, machine-based age, tomorrow's workers must depend more on their own knowledge and skills. They have to manage their own control systems, supervise themselves, and take upon themselves the responsibility to upgrade. They must be disciplined enough to think on their own and to seek to excel without someone breathing down their neck. Workers in the new economy cannot be content with just problem solving and perfecting the known. They must be enterprising and innovative, always seeking new ways of doing the job, to create the extra value, the extra edge.[24]

Today, because competence in English is no longer just a competitive advantage, many countries are trying to teach their children English. It is a basic skill that many children want to acquire in the 21st century. . . . If one is to succeed, one will need a mastery of English, because it is the language of business, science, diplomacy, and academia.[25]

CHAPTER 7

The Future of Geopolitics and Globalization

What are some of the biggest problems that the world faces over the next decade? What are Russia's long-term prospects? Will Brazil, Russia, India, and China—the so-called BRIC countries—gain influence as a bloc over time? What lessons have you learned from the global financial crisis? What opportunities and challenges does globalization present? What must individuals, companies, and countries do to succeed in a globalizing world? Is globalization reversible? This chapter offers Lee Kuan Yew's direct and penetrating answers to these questions.

What are some of the biggest problems that the world faces over the next decade?

First, there is the eurozone. If the Greek debt crisis is not handled properly, it will affect Portugal, Spain, and Italy. Then you have a chain reaction that harms not only the economies of Europe, but also those of the U.S. and China.

Second is the perennial problem of North Korea. A young man, Kim Jong-un, has taken over and is trying to show the world that he is as bold and adventurous as his predecessors.

Third is Japan's stagnation, which indirectly affects the whole of the Asia-Pacific. The aging of its society has prevented its economy from taking off. Japan is not accepting migrants because it wants to maintain a pure-blooded population.

Fourth is the chance of a conflict in the Middle East over the bomb that Iran is developing, which would have a catastrophic impact on markets. Iran's nuclear program is the challenge that the world is most likely to bungle. China and Russia are unlikely to enforce UN sanctions, and if Iran feels like they will continue not to enforce them, it will be encouraged to continue building a bomb. At some point Israel has to decide, whether with or without U.S. support, whether to try and destroy Iran's hardened underground shelters. If Iran gets the bomb, Saudi Arabia will buy the bomb from Pakistan, the Egyptians will buy the bomb from someone, and then you have a nuclearized Middle East. Then it is only a matter of time before there is a nuclear explosion in the region.[1]

What are Russia's long-term prospects?

Russia's future is no different than it was 10 years ago or even 20 years ago, when the Soviet Union collapsed, except that it has lost its hold on energy resources in the Caucasus and Kazakhstan. It has been unable to develop an economy that generates wealth independent of exports of energy and natural resources.

The Russian population is declining. It is not clear why, but alcoholism plays a role; so do pessimism, a declining fertility rate, and a declining life expectancy. Vladimir Putin's challenge is to give Russians a hopeful outlook for the future: stop drinking, work hard, build good families, and have more children.

Siberia and Vladivostok are filling up with more and more Chinese. The lands on the bend of the Amur River will be repopulated by Chinese. Russians may suddenly decide that the future is worth living and bring more children into the world to reverse this demographic trend, but I do not see that shift occurring in the near future.[2]

They would do enormously better if they could get their system right. Their system is not functioning . . . because it has gone haywire. They have lost control over the various provinces. . . . They have got an enormous nuclear arsenal, but what else? Their army is a very different army now. . . . Their population is declining. . . .

Every year more Russians die than Russians are born because people are not optimistic. In America, people are optimistic and say I will bring a child into the world. But when your life is so harsh, and from time to time it gets better when the oil price goes up, but that is momentary, you have a different view of the future.[3]

Will Brazil, Russia, India, and China—the so-called BRIC countries—gain influence as a bloc over time?

As a counterweight, yes—they will be able to prevent excesses by the Americans and the Europeans—but otherwise no. They are different countries on different continents that happen to be growing faster than other combinations of countries on those continents, so somebody said: why not bring them all together and make them into a global force? Sure, China will buy soybeans from Brazil. It is a growing country that needs resources and can pay for them. But the Chinese and Indians do not share the same dreams.[4]

Will the ASEAN countries gain influence as a bloc over time?

Yes, but very slowly, because they have not internalized the idea of having a common market, combining resources, and inviting investments into different parts of ASEAN [the Association of Southeast Asian Nations] depending on those parts' comparative advantages. They also lack confidence. Thailand is in some trouble over Thaksin Shinawatra and the monarchy. Vietnam remains very wary of China. Cambodia will take a long time to recover. Burma looks like it will open up this time, but think of its starting point: it has been closed for so long that nothing can make it worse.[5]

To remain at the center of East Asia's economic and political evolution, ASEAN must integrate more closely and with urgency. Otherwise, it will be marginalized. . . . ASEAN lacks strategic weight.[6]

Placed between the giants of China and India, ASEAN countries have to combine their markets to compete and be relevant as a region. There is no other choice.[7]

What lessons have you learned from the global financial crisis?

The global financial crisis was caused by excesses of the liberal system of regulations and the belief that a completely free market will allow enormous innovation and allocate capital to the most profitable enterprises with the highest returns. Once the Federal Reserve Chairman decided it was not necessary to regulate derivatives and supervise them, the fuse was lit. Once you find that you can mash up a lot of good and bad assets in one bundle and pass on your risk all around Europe and other parts of the world, you have started something like a Ponzi scheme which must come to an end sometime. . . . The business of a person in a financial institution is to make the biggest profit for himself, so just condemning the bankers and the profit takers does not make sense. You have allowed these rules, and they work within these rules.[8]

Free enterprise has brought about this crisis. . . . Governments have to carry the main burden and put the system right, and then allow private enterprise to pick up and carry on. But if, having put money into these banks and all these other enterprises, you then say you cannot pay out bonuses in such large sums, nor your stock options, then you will change the nature of the American free-enterprise system. It has worked well because you reward the people who make the company successful.[9]

We know such a recession must come from time to time. It is in the nature of the free markets of the western world that our economy is plugged into. People and systems tend to be carried away by exuberance. Investors get greedy and rush in to buy, believing that prices will only go up. When prices collapse, investors find they have lost huge sums. Despair and depression then set in.[10]

Prior to the current economic crisis the world did not challenge the Washington consensus that the Anglo-Saxon economic model is the most efficient for the allocation of financial resources to produce the highest return. However, the U.S. market model is no longer considered ideal. China is confident that it is better for the government to maintain control of and manage its economy. China will now also be slower to open its closed capital markets to avoid large inflows and outflows of speculative foreign currencies.[11]

Only large continental countries with huge populations like China's and India's can ramp up their domestic consumption to avoid being much affected by the current economic turmoil.[12]

What opportunities and challenges does globalization present?

One phase in human history has ended. The new one promises to be exciting. The move that triggered off a globalized market began in March 1991, when the National Science Foundation privatized the Internet, without quite realizing what a powerful instrument it would turn out to be for increasing productivity, enabling people and businesses to reach out to others across national boundaries, and to create a global intellectual community and a global marketplace.[13]

Economic power will be spread over many centers across the globe. They are "cities at the intersection," where people, ideas, and capital from various geographic regions meet, interact, and influence each other continually. These are the birthplaces of new knowledge, products, and services.[14]

Globalization's power was first demonstrated in the stock markets ten years ago, in July 1997, with the onset of the Asian financial crisis. Within days, all of the region's emerging markets were affected. . . . The ultimate threat to human survival is global warming and climate change. The habitats of millions, maybe billions, of people may be damaged. . . . The scramble for the riches under the ice is on. . . . If sea levels rise to inundate many millions of people, and if glaciers in the Himalayas, Tibet, and the Andes melt away, leaving more millions without enough water, there will be no "life as usual."[15]

It is technology, the human conquest of nature, that has changed the world forever, more so than all the changes in political and ideological spheres. . . . What will affect your generation's lives more profoundly than any other factor is the increasing speed of scientific and technological change. Your lives will become healthier and longer because the human genome has been mapped. There will be a flowering of discoveries in biotechnology over the next few decades. . . . There will be more food and goods for consumption worldwide. Trade and investments will expand globally as consumer societies thrive in more and more emerging countries. . . . More people make for more economic growth, more prosperity. But more people worldwide also build up grave problems: earth warming, rising sea levels, melting ice caps as carbon dioxide and greenhouse gases in the air change climates throughout the world. With a greater density of people, there will be more friction and conflicts as they fight for the same finite space in the world and for its limited resources, especially oil. There are other deep and abiding problems: AIDS, drug smuggling, illegal migration, global mafias. They are part and parcel of the globalized world, like global terrorism.[16]

The present world is as full of promise as of perils. New technologies, instant communications, and fast transportation have integrated the world. Everybody knows what is going on around them in the world. Migrations have been massive. Hundreds of millions from the poorer countries are moving into the wealthier countries in search of a better life. Great changes are taking place. The old established powers, the U.S. and the EU [European Union], have to accommodate new emerging powers such as China, India, Russia, and Brazil. Many other developing countries . . . are trying hard to catch up. Meanwhile, earth warming goes on as more carbon dioxide is released every day. Climate change will alter our habitat profoundly, in ways we cannot foresee.[17]

The rapid technological advancements of the past few years have greatly accelerated globalization. With quantum leaps in telecommunications and innovations in information technology like the Internet, the world has become a much smaller place. Physical distance, time differences, and national borders are no longer barriers to the free flow of information. It is now no longer necessary to travel long distances to find new ideas. Vast amounts of information can be transmitted instantaneously at the touch of the keyboard from anywhere, and at any time. This trend in IT [information technology] revolution will alter the nature of societies. It will transform the way we live, learn, work, and use leisure time. . . . Those countries that keep out advances of technology because of its undesirable by-products will be losers. For better or for worse, we have to seize the opportunities offered by the IT revolution, but try to minimize its harmful side effects. . . . People must stay abreast of the state-of-the-art technology, but must never lose their core values. Science and technology are decisive in determining future progress. But they should not be allowed to break up families that have to imbue children with a strong sense of social responsibility and the conscience to distinguish between right and wrong.[18]

Before WWII, international trade was most free within the boundaries of each of the empires, the American, British, various European, and Japanese. There were trade barriers between these imperial blocs. The Americans were determined to dissolve these empires after WWII. GATT [the General Agreement on Tariffs and Trade] was designed to facilitate cross-border trade in goods and services without the unifying control of an imperial center. It succeeded brilliantly. . . . But no one foresaw that technological advances in communications and transportation would lead to the growth and proliferation of multinational corporations that are able to expand the production and sale of goods followed by services, across national boundaries, and market them to all parts of the world. . . . Globalization, especially after the developments in the IT sector, has led to developed countries needing more talent. They have relaxed immigration rules and increased the mobility of talent in the developing world. . . . Human talent is at present the most scarce and valuable resource for creating wealth in the knowledge economy. . . . A negative result of globalization is the widening of the inequality between the highly educated and the less educated, between urban and rural incomes, and between coastal and inland provinces. The highly educated can move between countries seeking the high rewards in the developed countries, especially in sectors like IT and the Internet. The less educated are not mobile and cannot get into the developed countries, where wages are higher. This is unavoidable in a world driven by market forces.[19]

There are no historical precedents on how to maintain peace

and stability and to ensure cooperation in a world of 160 nation-states. And the age of instant communications and swift transportation, with technology growing exponentially, makes this problem very complex. In one interdependent, interrelated world, the decline in the relative dominance of the leaders of the two blocs increases the likelihood of a multipolar world, and with it the difficulties of multilateral cooperation.[20]

What must individuals, companies, and countries do to succeed in a globalizing world?

At the Forbes Global CEO conference on entrepreneurship, technology, and business leadership in the 21st century, I asked myself: what is the difference between these factors in the past and at present? In their fundamentals, neither entrepreneurship nor business leadership has changed. What has changed, and changed beyond recognition, is technology. Technology requires entrepreneurs and business leaders to think and act globally. They cannot avoid collaborating with, or competing against, others internationally. An entrepreneur wins or loses in competition against all others in his line of business, whether they are national or foreign players, because all players will be able to enter his national domain and compete against him. As long as competition was confined within national boundaries, each country was able to nurture its national champions, and they developed different styles of entrepreneurship and business leadership, resulting in different corporate cultures. . . . In today's globalized environment, brought about by the IT revolution and the WTO [World Trade Organization], is this possible? I believe it is infinitely more difficult for nations to create incubators for nurturing such national champions.[21]

The great challenge today is to adjust to the tectonic shift in the global economic balance. There will be a dramatic transformation in the decades ahead as China fully competes in the world economy as a member of the WTO. And India will not be left out. . . . Our way forward is to upgrade our levels of education, skills, knowledge, and technology. Lifelong learning is a must for everyone in this knowledge economy, with rapidly changing technology. Those who are not well-educated and cannot retrain to be computer literate, or learn new skills and acquire new knowledge every five to ten years, will find it harder to get jobs in convenient factories, because such factories will not be economic in Singapore.[22]

To succeed, Singapore must be a cosmopolitan center, able to attract, retain, and absorb talent from all over the world. We cannot keep the big companies out of the local league. Whether we like it or not, they are entering the region. The choice is simple. Either we have a first-class airline, a first-class shipping line, and a first-class bank, or we decline. One of the things we did in the early years was to buck the third world trend by inviting the multinational corporations, and we succeeded. Now, we must buck the third world trend to be nationalistic. We must be international in our outlook and practices. . . . Our own talent must be nurtured to come up to world standards by exposure and interaction with their foreign peers. Some of our best have been attracted away by leading American corporations. This is part of the global marketplace.[23]

In an era of rapid technological change, Americans have shown that those countries with the largest number of start-ups, especially in the IT industry, which venture capitalists finance, will be winners in this next phase. . . . Japanese, Koreans, and other East Asians have to accept some fundamental cultural changes to compete in a globalized marketplace. Those whose cultures help them to absorb and embrace talented people of different cultures to be part of the new corporate culture will have an advantage. Japanese and East Asians are ethnocentric, close-knit societies. They do not easily absorb foreigners into their midst. There has to be a fundamental change in cultural attitudes before Japanese and other East Asians can compete with the Americans who, because of their different history, easily absorb peoples of different cultures and religions into their corporate teams.[24]

The digital revolution and the convergence of communications, computers, and the media require more from us than simply copying the software innovations of the developed countries. Our enterprising young people must be given the space and scope to create businesses for themselves. The government must facilitate the venture-capital funds. We have followed a safe, structured approach. Now, our talented young have to dispense with the safety net as they go on their own. Many will stumble and fall, but they must pick themselves up and try again. The process of opening up may make our society more unruly. The gravest challenge will be to protect the values we cherish. . . . If you want to thrive in the modern world, then you must not be afraid.[25]

Technology and globalization have created a more level playing field. Because goods and services can be manufactured or produced anywhere, this has reduced the traditional competitive advantages of geographic location, climate, and natural resources. All countries can harness information technology and air transportation and join the global trading community in goods and services. It helps to close the gap between advantaged and disadvantaged countries. But one "X" factor remains a key differentiator, especially for developing countries: that is ethical leadership. . . . A clean, efficient, rational, and predictable government is a competitive advantage.[26]

Is globalization reversible?

Globalization cannot be reversed, because the technologies that made globalization inevitable cannot be uninvented. In fact, better and cheaper transportation and communications will further advance the forces of globalization.[27]

Will the international order collapse? Can it? Can the world afford to allow it to collapse and go into anarchy? . . . This interconnected world is not going to become disconnected. . . . The problems will become more acute the other way: overpopulation, earth warming, and displacement of millions, maybe billions of people. . . . It scares me, because many world leaders have not woken up to the peril that their populations are in. This melting ice cap. I expected great consternation! What would happen to this earth? But no. Has it triggered emergency meetings to do something about this? Earth warming, the glaciers melting away? . . . It is not an election issue. . . . Leave it to the next president. . . . You can ameliorate this problem. But you cannot solve it. Because our dependency on energy will only grow. . . . I do not see any tribal leader, any democratic leader, any dictator telling his people, "We are going to forgo growth. We are going to consume less. Travel less. Live a more spartan life, and we will save the earth."[28]

There is no viable alternative to global integration. Protectionism disguised as regionalism will sooner or later lead to conflicts and wars between the regional blocs as they compete for advantage in non-bloc areas, like the oil countries of the Gulf. Globalism is the only answer that is fair, acceptable, and will uphold world peace.[29]

The Future of Democracy

What is the role of government? What is the role of a leader? How responsive should a leader be to popular opinion? What are the requirements for democracy? What are the risks of democracy? What is the proper balance between law and order? What is the proper balance between competitiveness and equality? In the following answers, Lee Kuan Yew presents the essence of his political philosophy as well as practical lessons from his leadership of Singapore.

What is the role of government?

Only an efficient and effective government can provide the framework in which peoples can fulfill their needs. People cannot satisfy
their fundamental needs by themselves. They need the support and
organization of a tribe, or of government, to achieve this. Modern
technology requires specialization in a wide range of disciplines. A
high-tech society needs so much knowledge and so many skills.[1]

The business of a government is to . . . make firm decisions so
that there can be certainty and stability in the affairs of the people.[2]

The art of government is utilizing to the maximum the limited
resources at the country's disposal.[3]

Our immediate task is to build up a society in which people will
be rewarded not according to the amount of property they own,
but according to their active contribution to society in physical or
mental labor. From each according to his or her ability. To each according to his or her worth and contribution to society.[4]

A good government is expected not only to carry on and maintain standards. It is expected to raise them. And it is ultimately in
the sphere of economics that results must be achieved. More jobs
must be created; more prosperity diffused amongst more people.[5]

It is the business of the government which has grown from the
ground to keep its representatives on the ground, to ensure that
long before a grievance or dissatisfaction reaches acuteness, reme-
dies are put into motion. It is necessary to keep in constant touch
with the people not only to know what their grievances are, but also

to conduct and organize them and inculcate in them social qualities which will be useful in the building up of society.[6]

Westerners have abandoned an ethical basis for society, believing that all problems are solvable by a good government. . . . In the West, especially after World War II, the government came to be seen as so successful that it could fulfill all the obligations that in less modern societies are fulfilled by the family. . . . In the East, we start with self-reliance. In the West today, it is the opposite. The government says give me a popular mandate and I will solve all society's problems.[7]

What is the role of a leader?

It is the duty of leaders to instill confidence in the people so that they will stand up to be counted. . . . No army, however brave, can win when its generals are weak. Leaders must have the ability to plan and chart the way ahead, and the fortitude to stay the course. . . . When they fight together against all odds and win, a bond will be forged between people and leaders, like the deep unshakeable feeling of trust between an army and its generals who have been in battle together.[8]

Your job as a leader is to inspire and to galvanize, not to share your distraught thoughts. You make your people dispirited if you do so.[9]

A corporate leader does not have to persuade his workers to follow him. There is a hierarchy in a corporation, and he drives his policies through the organization. His job is to satisfy his customers and his shareholders. A political leader, however, must paint his vision of their future to his people, then translate that vision into policies which he must convince the people are worth supporting, and finally galvanize them to help him in their implementation.[10]

The test of leadership lies not merely in echoing fears and doubts, especially when these fears and doubts, however real, are capable of solution and of being rendered irrational and unfounded. As leaders of our various communities, we recognize the existence of these anxieties, but we have to take the lead in exorcising them. We cannot afford to passively let things drift. We have to take the lead in public thinking. After having drawn attention to the interests of our communities that require special protection, we must formulate solutions which will safeguard these interests and advance the common good.[11]

You either have the talent or you do not. My job is to find out, quickly, whether a person responsible for the fate of over 2 million Singaporeans has got it in him or her. If he or she does not, I am wasting my time. . . . Whether you teach a person how to play golf, or a dog how to be a sniffer of drugs, the first thing you must know is: has he or she got it?[12]

The most significant imprint we can leave is not by hanging on to office, but through the way we hand over the power to govern. We have exercised power as trustees for the people, with an abiding sense of our fiduciary responsibility. . . . When those in office regard the power vested in them as a personal prerogative, they inevitably enrich themselves, promote their families, and favor their friends. The fundamental structures of the modern state are eroded, like the supporting beams of a house after termites have attacked them. Then the people have to pay dearly and long for the sins and crimes of their leaders. Our future stability and progress depend on those succeeding us being imbued with this same sense of trusteeship, this awareness that to abuse the authority and power that they are entrusted with is to betray a trust. By handing over power whilst we are still alert and fully in charge, we are able to ensure that our successors have the basic attributes to be entrusted with power. It is feckless to hang on and to have power wrested from us when we have become feeble. Then we shall have no say over who our successors are.[13]

A nation is great not by its size alone. It is the will, the cohesion, the stamina, the discipline of its people, and the quality of their leaders which ensure it an honorable place in history.[14]

The history of a people is not decided in one or two election defeats or election victories. It is a long and relentless process not dependent on persons and personalities, but on the political and social and national forces at work within a given milieu. And it is only a question of whether one can analyze and decipher and discern the forces in play and calculate the resultant direction of all these forces. They are factors more enduring, more decisive than all the slogans that people or politicians or trade unionists can coin.[15]

Whatever the twists and turns of events in the immediate present, the relentless logic of geography and the force of historical, ethnic, and economic forces must prevail. . . . We must not go against what is historically inevitable. This does not mean that we passively wait for history to unfold itself. We must actively strive to accelerate the process of history.[16]

How responsive should a leader be to popular opinion?

I learned to ignore criticism and advice from experts and quasi-experts, especially academics in the social and political sciences. They have pet theories on how a society should develop to approximate their ideal, especially how poverty should be reduced and welfare extended. I always try to be correct, not politically correct.[17]

What the Western world does not understand is that at the end of the day, I am not worried by how they judge me. I am worried by how the people I have governed judge me.[18]

I do not take anything all that seriously. If I did, I would be quite a sick man. A number of foolish things will be said about you. If you take them all seriously, you will get quite demented.[19]

One has got to get over the temptation of the news media capturing one's soul. Never mind what the news media say.[20]

Government, to be effective, must at least give the impression of enduring, and a government which is open to the vagaries of the ballot box—when the people who put their crosses in the ballot boxes are not illiterate but semi-literate, which is worse—is a government which is already weakened before it starts to govern.[21]

My idea of popular government is that you do not have to be

popular all the time when you are governing. . . . There are moments when you have to be thoroughly unpopular. But at the end of your term, you should have brought about sufficient benefits so that the people realize what you did was necessary and will vote for you again. That is the basis on which I have governed. If you want to be popular all the time, you will misgovern.[22]

I have never been overconcerned or obsessed with opinion polls or popularity polls. I think a leader who is, is a weak leader. If you are concerned with whether your rating will go up or down, then you are not a leader. You are just catching the wind . . . you will go where the wind is blowing. . . . Between being loved and feared, I have always believed Machiavelli was right. If nobody is afraid of me, I am meaningless. When I say something . . . I have to be taken very seriously. . . . What the crowd thinks of me from time to time, I consider totally irrelevant. . . . The whole ground can be against, but if I know this is right, I set out to do it, and I am quite sure, given time, as events unfold, I will win over the ground. . . . My job as a leader is to make sure that before the next elections, enough has developed and disclosed itself to the people to make it possible for me to swing them around.[23]

What are the requirements for democracy?

Pakistan, Indonesia, and Burma are grim reminders that the democratic state is not something which will look after itself just by the setting up of a democratic constitution.[24]

What is our job in a democratic society? First, to mobilize opinion. . . . We have got to get everybody to prepare his mind to bear on these things, or as many people as possible, to argue and work out where we are going, where certain policies will lead us.[25]

A democratic society does not run itself automatically. It requires two things to succeed. First, there must be an interested and vigilant electorate to choose, and then to control by the force of public opinion, the politicians it elects to manage the country's affairs. Second, a democratic society must have honest and able political parties to give it a choice of alternative leaderships.[26]

Whether Singapore succeeds as a thriving democracy with an honest administration, or sags into disrepair and drifts into dictatorship with an administration riddled with corruption, depends upon whether there are enough men and women with education and training prepared to come out to do their share rather than see the country go down.[27]

In a democratic society, it is not enough just to sit back and watch the champions in the rings slog it out. Your unions, your officials, your members, and every one of you must take a stand, for by taking a stand, you will make the battle less costly and less painful and success even more certain. For if the battle is lost . . . then you, your unions, your academic rights, and academic freedom will all become so many empty words.[28]

Citizens must be prepared to support the leaders they voted for by making the effort and accepting the discipline and sacrifices necessary to achieve agreed objectives. The less the effort and sacrifice people are prepared for, the less the economic growth. The looser the social discipline and the more diffuse the consensus, the weaker will be the performance and the lower the productivity.[29]

It is fundamental to the working of the democratic system that important issues are placed before the people by all those contesting elections. . . . And whoever is chosen to represent the people is expected to implement faithfully the mandate that has been given to them. This is the essence of the democratic system.[30]

What are the risks of democracy?

One person, one vote is a most difficult form of government. From time to time, the results can be erratic. People are sometimes fickle. They get bored with stable, steady improvements in life, and in a reckless moment, they vote for a change for change's sake.[31]

So long as you run this one person, one vote, the easiest of appeals that can be made to the ground are the simple, emotional ones, not economic development and progress and all these other things they do not understand, but simple things: pride in race, in language, in religion, in culture.[32]

Parliamentary democracy of one person, one vote will work only if people choose rationally from the alternatives they are offered in an election. The ideal is never offered. The voter is faced with a limited choice of alternatives. He must reconcile his hopes and aspirations with the parties offered him. The democratic system breaks down if people make a choice which is irrational, as they did time after time in France after WWII until [Charles] de Gaulle swept aside the Fourth Republic. The system also fails if none of the parties contesting offers a rational choice, as in Indonesia between 1949 and 1959 until President Sukarno swept aside Parliament and installed himself as "guider" of democracy.[33]

What are we all seeking? A form of government that will be comfortable because it meets our needs, is not oppressive, and maximizes our opportunities. And whether you have one person, one vote or some people, one vote, or other people, two votes, those are forms which should be worked out. I am not intellectually convinced that one person, one vote is the best. We practice it because that is what the British bequeathed us, and we have not really found a need to challenge that. But I am convinced, personally, that we would have a better system if we gave every person over the age of 40 who has a family two votes, because he or she is likely to be more careful, voting also for his or her children. He or she is more likely to vote in a serious way than a capricious young person under 30. . . . At the same time, once a person gets beyond 65, then it is a problem. Between the ages of 40 and 60 is ideal, and at 60 they should go back to one vote, but that will be difficult to arrange.[34]

One person, one vote, on the basis of the Western parliamentary democratic system . . . is workable within certain limitations. You have such things as fixed attitudes. Of what is right and what is wrong. Well, your population automatically responds to certain basic stimuli, but you let a free-for-all take place, and in every one of the newly emergent countries, they face trouble immediately after independence is won. That is one of the problems of an emergent society. Authority has got to be exercised. And when authority is not backed by position, prestige, or usage, then it has to defend actively against challenge.[35]

What is the proper balance between law and order?

The day [Mikhail] Gorbachev said to the masses in Moscow: do not be afraid of the KGB, I took a deep breath. This man is a real genius, I said. . . . He is sitting on top of a terror machine that holds the damn pile together, and he says: do not be afraid. He must have a tremendous formula to democratize. Until I met him, and I found him completely bewildered by what was happening around him. He had jumped into the deep end of the pool without learning how to swim.

I understood Deng Xiaoping when he said: if 200,000 students have to be shot, shoot them, because the alternative is China in chaos for another 100 years. . . . Deng understood, and he released it stage by stage. Without Deng, China would have imploded.[36]

The rule of law talks of habeas corpus, freedom, the right of association and expression, of assembly, of peaceful demonstration: nowhere in the world today are these rights allowed to be practiced without limitations, for blindly applied, these ideals can work toward the undoing of organized society. For the acid test of any legal system is not the greatness or the grandeur of its ideal concepts, but whether, in fact, it is able to produce order and justice in the relationships between person and person, and between person and the state. To maintain this order with the best degree of tolerance and humanity is a problem. . . . In a settled and established society, law appears to be a precursor of order. . . . But the hard realities of keeping the peace between person and person, and between authority and the individual, can be more accurately described if the phrase were inverted to "order and law," for without order, the operation of law is impossible. Order having been established, and the rules having become enforceable in a settled society, only then is it possible to work out human relationships between subject and subject, and subject and the state in accordance with predetermined rules of law. And when a state of increasing disorder and defiance of authority cannot be checked by the rules then existing . . . drastic rules have to be forged to maintain order so that the law can continue to govern human relations. The alternative is to surrender order for chaos and anarchy.[37]

All colonial territories that have gained their independence since the end of World War II have equipped themselves with emergency laws. . . . Good government does not depend upon the absence of these powers. It depends upon the wise, judicious, and discriminate use of them by the representatives elected by and answerable to the people.[38]

What is the proper balance between competitiveness and equality?

To be successful, society must maintain a balance between nurturing excellence and encouraging the average to improve. There must be both cooperation and competition between people in the same society.[39]

If everybody gets the same rewards, as they do under communism with their iron rice bowl, nobody strives to excel; society will not prosper, and progress will be minimal. That led to the collapse of the communist system. On the other hand, in a highly competitive society where winners get big prizes and losers paltry ones, there will be a great disparity between the top and the bottom layers of society, as in America. . . . At the end of the day, the basic problem of fairness in society will need to be solved. But first, we have to create the wealth. To do that, we must be competitive and have a good dose of the "yang." If we have too much of the "yin" and over-redistribute the incomes of the successful, then we will blunt their drive to excel and succeed, and may lose too many of our able, who will move to other countries where they are not so heavily taxed. On the other hand, if too many at the lower end feel left out, then our society will become divisive and fractious, and cohesiveness will be lost. Communism has failed. The welfare state of Western democracies has also failed.

There is a continual need to balance between a successful, competitive society, and a cohesive, compassionate one. That requires judgment, to strike a bargain or social contract. Each society must arrive at that optimum point for itself. Between the two ends, the highly competitive and the excessively equal, lies a golden mean. This point will move with time and changing values.[40]

I can best explain the need for balance between individual competition and group solidarity by using the metaphor of the oriental yin and yang symbol. . . . The more yang (male) competitiveness in society, the higher the total performance. If winner takes all, competition will be keen, but group solidarity will be weak. The more yin (female) solidarity, with rewards evenly distributed, the greater the group solidarity, but the weaker the total performance because of reduced competition. . . . We have arranged help, but in such a way that only those who have no other choice will seek it. This is the opposite of attitudes in the West, where liberals actively encourage people to demand entitlements with no sense of shame, causing an explosion of welfare costs.[41]

In one generation (1965 to 1990), we made it from third world to first. The next 20 years until 2010, Singapore acquired the poise and polish of a vibrant and lively city. . . . To build such a Singapore, we need an exceptionally strong government, with the ablest, the toughest, and most dedicated of leaders. We headhunt for them, test them out in heavy responsibilities. Only such leaders can keep the economy growing and create good jobs and generate the revenue to pay for the equipment and training of our third-generation Singapore Armed Forces [SAF]. This 3-G

[3rd generation] SAF provides the security and confidence of our people and of foreign investors, assured that we can more than defend ourselves. If there is insecurity, there will be fewer investments. That means a poorer people and instability.

To maintain social cohesion, we buffer the lowest 20% to 25%, the weaker achievers, from the tough competition of the marketplace. . . . We support the lower-income workers with extra income. . . . All this aims for a fair and just society.[42]

CHAPTER 9

How Lee Kuan Yew Thinks

What are your most fundamental strategic principles? How do you approach strategic thinking and policymaking? What personal and professional experiences have shaped that approach? What strategic paradigms have shaped that approach? What role should history play in strategic thinking and policymaking? What role should clarity play in strategic thinking and policymaking? How has your view of why societies progress affected your strategic thinking? How has your view of why societies stagnate or regress affected your strategic thinking? What qualities define a successful leader? What are the most common public policy mistakes that leaders make? Which leaders do you admire and why? How do you wish to be remembered? Lee Kuan Yew's answers to these questions reveal much about the principles and worldview that have shaped his political choices.

What are your most fundamental strategic principles?

Human beings, regrettable though it may be, are inherently vicious and have to be restrained from their viciousness.[1]

We may have conquered space, but we have not learned to conquer our own primeval instincts and emotions that were necessary for our survival in the Stone Age, not in the space age.[2]

One of the most tragic personal events was when Mr. Nehru faced the agony of disillusionment in his basic, fundamental belief. That, in fact, power politics in Asia is as old as the first tribes that emerged, and that, whether we like it or not, if we are to survive and maintain our separate identities, it is necessary that we should learn what is in the joint interest at any single time of a group of nations.[3]

I have always thought that humanity was animal-like, while Confucian theory says that it can be improved. I am not sure it can be, but it can be trained, it can be disciplined. . . . You can make a left-hander write with his or her right hand, but you cannot really change his or her natural-born instinct.[4]

It is assumed that all men and women are equal or should be

equal. . . . But is equality realistic? If it is not, to insist on equality must lead to regression.[5]

One of the facts of life is that no two things are ever equal, either in smallness or in bigness. Living things are never equal. Even in the case of identical twins, one comes out before the other and takes precedence over the other. So it is with human beings, so it is with tribes, and so it is with nations.[6]

Human beings are not born equal. They are highly competitive. Systems like Soviet and Chinese communism have failed, because they tried to equalize benefits. Then nobody works hard enough, but everyone wants to get as much as, if not more than, the other person.[7]

I started off believing all men and women are equal. . . . I now know that is the most unlikely thing ever to have been because millions of years have passed over evolution, people have scattered across the face of this earth, been isolated from each other, developed independently, had different intermixtures between races, peoples, climates, soils. . . . This is something which I have read, and I tested against my observations. We read many things. The fact that it is in print and repeated by three, four authors does not make it true. They may all be wrong. But through my own experience . . . I concluded: yes, there is a difference.[8]

In any given society, of the 1,000 babies born, there are so many percent near-geniuses, so many percent average, so many percent morons. . . . It is the near-geniuses and the above-average who ultimately decide the shape of things to come. . . . We want an equal society. We want to give everybody equal opportunities. But, in the back of our minds, we never deceive ourselves that two human beings are ever equal in their stamina, in their drive, in their dedication, in their innate ability.[9]

Friedrich Hayek's book *The Fatal Conceit: Errors of Socialism* expressed with clarity and authority what I had long felt but was unable to express, namely the unwisdom of powerful intellects, including Albert Einstein, when they believed that a powerful brain can devise a better system and bring about more "social justice" than what historical evolution, or economic Darwinism, has been able to work out over the centuries.[10]

No single power, no single religion, no single ideology can conquer the world, or remake it in its own image. The world is too diverse. Different races, cultures, religions, languages, and histories require different paths to democracy and the free market. Societies in a globalized world—interconnected by satellite, television, Internet, and travel—will influence and affect each other. What social system best meets the needs of a people at a particular stage in their development will be settled by social Darwinism.[11]

How do you approach strategic thinking and policymaking?

I would describe myself, in perhaps European terms, as between socialist and conservative. I would put myself as a liberal. As someone who believes in equal opportunities so that everybody gets an equal chance to do his best, and with a certain compassion to ensure that the failures do not fall through the floor. . . . I want to run the system as efficiently as possible, but make allowances for those who will not be doing well because nature did not give them enough, or they cannot make that extra effort. . . . I am a liberal in the classical sense of that word, in that I am not fixated on a particular theory of the world or of society. I am pragmatic. I am prepared to look at the problem and say, all right, what is the best way to solve it that will produce the maximum happiness and well-being for the maximum number of people?[12]

My upbringing in a three-generation family made me an unconscious Confucianist. It seeps into you, the Confucianist belief that society works best where every man aims to be a gentleman. The ideal is a *junzi,* a gentleman. . . . That means he does not do evil, he tries to do good, he is loyal to his father and mother, faithful to his wife, brings up his children well, treats his friends properly, and he is a good, loyal citizen of his emperor. . . . The underlying philosophy is that for a society to work well, you must have the interests of the mass of the people, that society takes priority over the interests of the individual. This is the primary difference with the American principle, the primary rights of the individual.[13]

When I travel . . . I am watching how a society, an administration, is functioning. Why are they good? . . . And the ideas come from not just reading. You can read about it, but it is irrelevant if you do not relate it to yourself . . . which I constantly do. . . . You must not overlook the importance of discussions with knowledgeable people. I would say that is much more productive than absorbing or running through masses of documents. Because in a short exchange, you can abstract from somebody who has immense knowledge and experience the essence of what he had gained.[14]

It is not by accident that we got here. Every possible thing that could have gone wrong, we tried to preempt. That is how we got here, that is why we have substantial reserves. Because if we do not have reserves, the moment we run into trouble . . . we have got nothing. All we have is this functioning organism which requires brains, specialized skills put together in a very intricate form, with inputs from many nations and their experts in financial services, manufacturing, tourism, all sorts of economic activities put together. It is not easy to replicate. I consider this to be the best contribution I can make, the most worthwhile thing to do.[15]

What personal and professional experiences have shaped that approach?

My thinking comes from my character. . . . I also have my life experiences. One meets a series of unforeseeable and unpredictable situations when your whole world collapses. Anyway, mine did. The British Empire was supposed to last another 1,000 years in Southeast Asia, but collapsed when the Japanese army came in 1942. I never thought they could conquer Singapore and push the British out. They did, and brutalized us, including me. . . . I learned about power long before Mao Zedong wrote that power came from the barrel of the gun. The Japanese demonstrated this; the British did not. They were at the tail end of empire when they did not have to use brute force. The British had superiority in technology, commerce, and knowledge. They built this big government house on a hill with Indian convict labor in 1868 to dominate the populations. . . . I learned how to govern, how you dominate the people, as the British did, and how the Japanese used their power.[16]

The Japanese invasion of Singapore was the single biggest political education of my life because, for three and a half years, I saw the meaning of power and how power and politics and government went together, and I also understood how people trapped in a power situation responded because they had to live. One day, the British were there, immovable, complete masters; next day, the Japanese, whom we had derided, mocked as short, stunted people with shortsighted squint eyes.[17]

When my senior Cabinet colleagues and I look back at our early hectic years of governing Singapore, we realize how much we have benefited from having gone through a very hard school. We met street thugs. Had we not become streetwise, we would have been clobbered. Like dogs which are closeted in a bungalow behind fences, we would have been run over when exposed to treacherous traffic. . . . A whole generation of Singaporeans, now all over 40 years old, was educated in a harsh political school. . . . Our children have no memories of troubled times from reckless opposition. A younger generation of ministers also missed this experience. Fierce combat made the older ministers what they are. Those amongst us who were weak, slow, or nervous became early casualties. Those present are the survivors of a Darwinian process of natural selection. We have keen survival instincts.[18]

What have I learned since 1973? Some more basic unchangeables about human beings and human societies, the ways in which they can be made to do better, and the ever-present danger of regression and even collapse. . . . I realize how very fragile a civilized society is. . . . I have also come to understand the insignificance of personal achievements. For at 60, more than at 50, comes the realization of the transient nature of all earthly glories and successes, and the ephemeral quality of sensory joys and pleasures, when compared to intellectual, moral, or spiritual satisfactions. . . . I have wondered how much of what I am is nature and how much was nurture? Would I have been a different person if I had not been tempered through the crucible of struggle? . . . Having taken life-and-death decisions and gone through one acute crisis after another, my perspectives, ambitions, and priorities have undergone a fundamental and, I believe, permanent, transformation. I may not have changed in my physical, mental, and emotional make-up, the hardware side. But the software side, my responses to God, glory, or gold, has been conditioned by my experiences. In other words, however capacious the hardware (nature), without the software (nurture), not much can be made of the hardware.[19]

What strategic paradigms have shaped that approach?

The final corroboration of logic and reasoning comes when they become practical realities.[20]

The acid test is in performance, not promises. The millions of dispossessed in Asia care not and know not of theory. They want a better life. They want a more equal, just society.[21]

Good sense and good economics require that we must always find practical, not doctrinaire, solutions to our problems of growth and development.[22]

My life is not guided by philosophy or theories. I get things done and leave others to extract the principles from my successful solutions. I do not work on a theory. Instead, I ask: what will make this work? If, after a series of solutions, I find that a certain approach worked, then I try to find out what was the principle behind the solution. So Plato, Aristotle, Socrates, I am not guided by them. . . . I am interested in what works. . . . Presented with the difficulty or major problem or an assortment of conflicting facts, I review what alternatives I have if my proposed solution does not work. I choose a solution which offers a higher probability of success, but if it fails, I have some other way. Never a dead end.[23]

We were not ideologues. We did not believe in theories as such. A theory is an attractive proposition intellectually. What we faced was a real problem of human beings looking for work, to be paid, to buy their food, their clothes, their homes, and to bring their children up. . . . I had read the theories and maybe half believed in them. But we were sufficiently practical and pragmatic enough not to be cluttered up and inhibited by theories. If a thing works, let us work it, and that eventually evolved into the kind of economy that we have today. Our test was: does it work? Does it bring benefits to the people? . . . The prevailing theory then was that multinationals were exploiters of cheap labor and cheap raw materials and would suck a country dry. . . . Nobody else wanted to exploit the labor. So why not, if they want to exploit our labor? They are welcome to it. . . . We were learning how to do a job from them, which we would never have learnt. . . . We were part of the process that disproved the theory of the development economics school, that this was exploitation. We were in no position to be fussy about highminded principles.[24]

Kim Dae-jung wrote in *Foreign Affairs* that "democracy is our destiny." They got him to write a counter article to my conversation with Fareed Zakaria, and they want me to reply. I do not think it is necessary. He makes assertive statements. Where are the concrete examples that these things are going to happen? If it is going to happen, why are they so excited about it? . . . The very fact that they are so vexed about it and try to demolish me shows a lack of faith in the inevitable outcome they predict. . . . If history is on their side, that liberal democracy is inevitable, then just ignore me. Do not give me publicity. Right? I do not believe that because a theory sounds good, looks logical on paper, or is presented logically, therefore that is the way it will work out. The final test is life. What happens in real life, what happens with people working in a society.[25]

I do not believe the American system is either desirable or affordable. I notice the British are trying to copy the Americans. . . . Because American officials release secrets, that is supposed to be the "in" thing. It shows that yours is a free society where if any ministers or courts suppress the truth, you feel it is your duty to leak it to the opposition. That is something new, and it is not proven. So when you tamper around with the fundamentals of society . . . the effects are in the next, and often after the next, generation. . . . Perhaps because I am conservative, because one is a proven tested system, the other is not proven, why not let the other chap prove it first? If . . . all the contentiousness leads to a great flourishing of scientific and technological discoveries and . . . great happiness and absence of real social problems, it would be stupid not to look into those possibilities for ourselves. . . . The final proof is what happens to the society.[26]

What role should history play in strategic thinking and policymaking?

History does not repeat itself in the same way each time, but certain trends and consequences are constants. If you do not know history, you think short term. If you know history, you think medium and long term.[27]

To understand the present and anticipate the future, one must know enough of the past, enough to have a sense of the history of a people. One must appreciate not merely what took place, but, more especially, why it took place and in that particular way. This is true of individuals, as it is for nations. The personal experience of a person determines whether he likes or hates certain things, welcomes them or fears them when they recur. So it is with nations: it is the collective memory of a people, the composite learning from past events which led to successes or disasters that makes a people welcome or fear new events, because they recognize parts in new events which have similarities with past experience. Young people learn best from personal experience. The lessons their elders have learned at great pain and expense can add to the knowledge of the young and help them to cope with problems and dangers they had not faced before; but such learning, second hand, is never as vivid, as deep, or as durable as that which was personally experienced.[28]

During the Vietnam War, the Americans found that their lack of historical depth of understanding of the people and the country was a serious disadvantage. American universities like Yale, Cornell, Stanford, and think tanks like the RAND Corporation quickly assembled top minds in cognate disciplines to develop this expertise. Had they done this before they were drawn into the Vietnam War, they might well have chosen not to draw the battle line in Vietnam, but in Cambodia.[29]

What role should clarity play in strategic thinking and policymaking?

What I want to discuss is the importance of simple, clear, written English. This is not simple. . . . Arthur Koestler rightly pointed out that if Hitler's speeches had been written, not spoken, the Germans would never have gone to war. . . . When you send me or send your minister a minute or a memo, or a draft that has to be published like the president's address, do not try to impress by big words. Impress by the clarity of your ideas. . . . I speak as a practitioner. If I had not been able to reduce complex ideas into simple words and project them vividly for mass understanding, I would not be here today.[30]

Many of my propositions may be controversial, but where it is a choice between platitudes and personal convictions, I feel it is my duty to state my convictions vigorously, for one great obstacle to a rapid and orderly political development of Malaya has been, and still is, the Malayan habit of ignoring unpalatable facts and avoiding unpleasant controversy.[31]

Only those count and matter who have the strength and courage of their convictions to stick up and stand up for what they believe in, for their people, for their country, regardless of what happens to them.[32]

How has your view of why societies progress affected your strategic thinking?

Civilizations emerge because human societies in a given condition respond to the challenge. Where the challenge is just about right . . . the human being flourishes.[33]

There are three basic essentials for [the] successful transformation of any society. First, a determined leadership . . . two, an administration which is efficient; and three, social discipline.[34]

You have got to believe in something. You are not just building houses in order that people can procreate and fill these houses up. . . . You do these things because you believe that, in the end, you will create a happy and healthy nation, a society in which people find fulfillment. . . . If you treat human beings just like animals, you just feed them, keep them sleek, well-exercised, healthy like dogs or cats, I do not think that it will work. Nations have gone through tremendous privations and hardships in order to achieve specific goals which have inspired and fired their imagination.[35]

One of the reasons why a privileged society based on the privilege of property and rank must give way to a society where people are rewarded according to their ability and their contribution to society is that it is only when people are encouraged to give their best that society progresses. No society has existed in history where all people were equal and obtained equal rewards. If that were to be practiced, and the lazy and the incompetent were paid as much as the industrious and the intelligent, it would end up by all the good people giving as little of themselves so as not to give more than their weaker brethren. But it is possible to create a society in which everybody is given not equal rewards, but equal opportunities, and where rewards vary not in accordance with the ownership of property, but with the worth of a person's contribution to that society. In other words, society should make it worth people's while to give their best to the country. This is the way to progress.[36]

I did not understand what a cosseted life would do to the spirit of enterprise of a people, diminishing their desire to achieve and succeed. I believed that wealth came naturally from wheat growing in the fields, orchards bearing fruit every summer, and factories turning out all that was needed to maintain a comfortable life. Only two decades later, when I had to make an outdated entrepôt economy feed a people, did I realize we needed to create the wealth before we can share it. And to create wealth, high motivation and incentives are crucial to drive a people to achieve, to take risks for profit, or there will be nothing to share.[37]

You must want. That is the crucial thing. Before you have, you must want to have. And to want to have means to be able, first, to perceive what it is you want; secondly, how to discipline and organize yourself in order to possess the things you want—the industrial sinews of our modern economic base; and thirdly, the grit and the stamina, which means cultural mutations in the way of life in large parts of the tropical areas of the world where the human being has never found it necessary to work in the summer, harvest before autumn, and save up for the winter. In large areas of the world, a cultural pattern is determined. . . . As long as that persists, nothing will ever emerge. And for it to emerge, there must be this desire between contending factions of the "have" nations to try and mold the "have-not" nations after their own selves.[38]

Let me put in a positive way what we want. First, a striving, acquisitive community. You cannot have people just striving for a nebulous ideal. They must have that desire to improve. . . . You must equate rewards to performance, because no two persons want to be the same. They want equal chances in order that they can show how one is better than the other. . . . Next, we want forward-looking good management. The old family business is one of the problems in Singapore. . . . And third, easy social mobility. One of the reasons contributing to Japanese and German recovery was that their defeated capitalists, managers, executives, engineers, and workers . . . were fired by a singleness of purpose: to put their country back on its feet.[39]

To optimize our opportunities, we must retain the vigor of our multi-racial-lingual-cultural-religious society. We have the advantage of all being educated in English in an age when English is the common language of the world and the Internet. However, we must not lose our basic strengths, the vitality of our original cultures and languages. . . . Realism and pragmatism are necessary to overcome new problems. Only those basics that have proved sound in the past should not be changed unless absolutely necessary. Amongst them are honesty and integrity, multi-racialism, equality of opportunities, meritocracy, fairness in rewards in accordance with one's contribution to society, avoidance of the buffet syndrome where, for a fixed price, you can take or eat as much as you want. That is why welfare and subsidies destroy the motivation to perform and succeed.[40]

In an established national society, one of the fundamental qualifications for joining that national society is an adequate knowledge of the unifying language of that society. It was this language qualification that ensured for the Americans that basic unifying force. Racially, the immigrants started as Germans, Italians,

Spaniards, and even Japanese. But the fact that the American state insisted on an adequate command of the American version of English before accepting the immigrants as citizens of the state ensured the unifying force of one common language in the people.[41]

Why did China's technological advance slow down and halt, just when the Renaissance was beginning in Europe? China's stagnation was caused by its arrogance and complacency. It refused to learn from the West. When the British emissary Lord Macartney arrived in Beijing in 1793, bringing with him the marvels of the industrial revolution, the Emperor Qian Long was not impressed. The great emperor told the English nobleman, "There is nothing we lack nor do we need any of your country's manufactures." The price China paid for this arrogance was 200 years of decline and decay, while Europe and America forged ahead. Two hundred years later, another Chinese leader, more thoughtful and practical, set out to undo the damage. Deng Xiaoping opened up China to the world in 1978.[42]

The Israelis are very smart. I asked a Bank of America president . . . why are the Jews so smart? . . . He emphasized how the good genes multiplied. He said the rabbi in any Jewish society was often the most intelligent and well-read, most learned of all because he has got to know Hebrew, he has got to know the Talmud, he has got to know various languages and so on. So the rabbi's children are much sought-after by successful Jews to bring the good genes into the family. That is how they multiply, the bright ones multiply. That sums it up.[43]

How has your view of why societies stagnate or regress affected your strategic thinking?

Britain did not have the critical mass numbers of people and size of country to remain among the first rank of nations with America and the Soviet Union. But it was not inevitable that the enterprise and the drive of Britons to achieve would be hobbled by welfarism, introduced in 1945 with the noblest of motives by the British Labor Party. Cradle-to-grave welfarism blunted the ambition of many budding entrepreneurs. Worse, high personal taxes dampened the desire of many to achieve wealth and success.[44]

The British used to make the great discoveries—steam engines, textile machines, and electric motors. They won many Nobel Prizes for science. However, they did not commercialize their discoveries. . . . Why this lack of capacity to commercialize their innovations? I believe it is because of their culture. Long years of empire over two centuries developed a society where old wealth and the landed gentry were held in high esteem. The new rich were regarded with some disdain. The bright aspired to be successful and admired for their intellectual skills as lawyers, doctors, professionals, people who used their brains and kept clean hands, not like engineers or people who worked hard and had to dirty their hands. . . . The new rich were not embraced in the upper reaches of society. Only their children could aspire to be welcomed after going through the necessary public schools and universities, and their new wealth had matured and become old wealth. . . . Circumstances and culture decide how entrepreneurial a people or a sub-group of them becomes. . . . These are the four salient features of America's entrepreneurial culture: (1) a national emphasis on personal independence and self-reliance, (2) respect for those starting new businesses, (3) acceptance of failure in entrepreneurial and innovation efforts, and (4) tolerance for a high degree of income disparity.[45]

What qualities define a successful leader?

Revolutionary situations throw up great leaders who demand blood, sweat, and tears; comfortable circumstances produce leaders who promise people an even easier life.[46]

From my empirical observation of people and leaders, I believe 70–80% of a person's capability, proclivities, temperament is genetic. The day you are conceived, at least 70% has already been fixed in the womb. If you are bound to be a capable person, you will grow into a capable person. If you are bound to be slow, you will be slow. Nothing can change that. . . . I do not believe, contrary to what American books say, that you can teach people to be leaders. I think you are a born leader or you are not a leader. You can teach a person to be a manager, but not a leader. They must have the extra drive, intellectual verve, an extra tenacity, and the will to overcome.[47]

It is a very tough job, especially in political leadership. Being a CEO or the general of an army is different. You do not have to persuade people who can say "boo" to you to get them on your side. When campaigning, no one has to listen to you at all. And when the campaign is over, people have to believe that you have got something for them that you can do that will make them cast their vote for you. It requires a totally different set of skills. Those skills can only be developed if you have a natural urge, a natural interest in people, in wanting to do something for them, which they can sense and feel. If you have not got that and you just want to be a great leader, try some other profession.[48]

I have spent 40 years trying to select people for big jobs. . . . I have gone through many systems, spoken to many CEOs. . . . I decided that Shell had the best system of them all, and the government switched from 40 attributes to three, which they called "helicopter qualities". . . . What are they? Powers of analysis; logical grasp of the facts; concentration on the basic points, extracting the principles. You score high marks in mathematics, you have got it. But that is not enough. . . . They must have a sense of reality of what is possible. But if you are just realistic, you become pedestrian, plebeian, you will fail. Therefore, you must be able to soar above the reality and say, "This is also possible"—a sense of imagination.[49]

Unless you want long periods of anarchy and chaos, you have to create a self-continuing power structure. Human beings should be equal. But they never are. Some can do more; some can give more of themselves than others. How do we anticipate that? Why is it that often we cannot? . . . The problem is that the human being is unable yet to assess this thing called "character." . . . It is amazing how many highly intelligent persons in the world make no contribution at all to the well-being of their fellow people. And it is this as yet unascertainable or, rather, as yet unmeasurable, quality called "character," which, plus your mental capacity or knowledge or discipline, makes for leadership. . . . In the established societies . . . all their leadership comes from a broad stratum of people who have gone to universities. It is so much better if . . . a person also goes through a systematic course of discipline, learns all the basic norms, what history has to offer and human experience has to offer, and then takes over that leadership.[50]

What are the most common public policy mistakes that leaders make?

Sometimes they succumb to hubris and overconfidence, and other times they miss a transformative opportunity when it arrives.[51]

Which leaders do you admire and why?

De Gaulle, Deng Xiaoping, Winston Churchill. De Gaulle because he had tremendous guts. His country was occupied. He was a one-star general, and he represented France. . . . When the British and the Americans recaptured North Africa, he went to Algeria and Algiers, and he saw a French general there, a four-star general. He said, "Giraud, you are a general of France. What is the American soldier doing outside protecting you?" He was a very tough-minded fellow. . . . He had guts and gumption. Deng was a great man because he changed China from a broken-backed state, which would have imploded like the Soviet Union, into what it is today, on the way to becoming the world's largest economy. Churchill, because any other person would have given up. But he said . . . "We will fight on the beaches. We will fight in the fields and in the streets. We will never surrender." To say that when your troops have been defeated . . . required an enormous amount of will and verve and determination not to yield to the Germans. . . . If you ask the Americans who they admire, they will say Roosevelt. But Roosevelt had power and the industrial might of America.[52]

Of all my Cabinet colleagues, it was Goh Keng Swee who made the greatest difference to the outcome for Singapore. He had a capacious mind and a strong character. When he held a contrary view, he would challenge my decisions and make me reexamine the premises on which they were made. As a result, we reached better decisions for Singapore. In the middle of a crisis, his analysis was always sharp, with an academic detachment and objectivity that reassured me. His robust approach to problems encouraged me to press on against seemingly impossible odds. . . . He was my troubleshooter. I settled the political conditions so that his tough policies we together formulated could be executed. . . . He mastered defense matters, read up the classics on strategy, Sun Tzu, Clausewitz, and Liddell Hart. He subscribed to military journals to know the latest in military weaponry. He sent me books and articles, sidelined and flagged, insisting that I must know enough to decide what I had to approve.[53]

How do you wish to be remembered?

I do not want to be remembered as a statesman. First of all, I do not classify myself as a statesman. I put myself down as determined, consistent, persistent. I set out to do something. I keep on chasing it until it succeeds. That is all. . . . Anybody who thinks he is a statesman needs to see a psychiatrist.[54]

I do not think I can decide how I will be remembered. I live my life in accordance to what I think is worth doing. I never wanted to be in politics. I wanted to be a lawyer and make a good living, to be a good advocate, but I was thrown into it as a result of all these political earthquakes that took place. So I was saddled with the responsibility, and I just have to be responsible to get the place going. . . . All I can do is to make sure that when I leave, the institutions are good, sound, clean, efficient, and there is a government in place which knows what it has got to do and is looking for a successive government of quality.[55]

I am not saying that everything I did was right, but everything I did was for an honorable purpose. I had to do some nasty things, locking fellows up without trial. Close the coffin, then decide. Then you assess me. I may still do something foolish before the lid is closed on me.[56]

CHAPTER 10

⊞

Conclusion

As Washington policymakers, foreign policy experts, business leaders, and informed citizens finish reading this brief volume, we are confident that they will do so with a clearer vision of the complexities and challenges that America will face in the next decade and beyond. As the title of the book suggests, Lee Kuan Yew has given the next president and the rest of us a reliable compass with which to navigate that world. Here, we conclude with a few of the strategic insights that we find most instructive from this quiet, articulate, supremely confident, yet remarkably modest man from whom we have learned so much.

1. It is China's intention to be the greatest power in the world. The policies of all governments toward China, especially neighboring countries, have already taken this into account. These governments are repositioning themselves because they know that

there will be consequences if they thwart China when its core interests are at stake. China can impose economic sanctions simply by denying access to its market of 1.3 billion people, whose incomes and purchasing power are increasing.

2. The ways in which Chinese superiority will be expressed will undoubtedly be quite different than in the earlier era. Take the current case of East Asia, where they have, obviously, established a dominant economic position in relations with their neighbors, and used that position including access to a market of 1.3 billion people and significant investments in other countries to their advantage. If states or enterprises do not accept China's position and pay appropriate deference, they are faced with the threat of being shut out of a rapidly growing market with 1.3 billion people.

3. Straight-line extrapolations from such a remarkable record are not realistic. China has more handicaps going forward and more obstacles to overcome than most observers recognize. Chief among these are their problems of governance: the absence of the rule of law, which in today's China is closer to the rule of the emperor; a huge country in which little emperors across a vast expanse exercise great local influence; cultural habits that limit imagination and creativity, rewarding conformity; a language that shapes thinking through epigrams and 4,000 years of texts that suggest everything worth saying has already been said,

and said better by earlier writers; a language that is exceedingly difficult for foreigners to learn sufficiently to embrace China and be embraced by its society; and severe constraints on its ability to attract and assimilate talent from other societies in the world.

4. He [Xi Jinping, the likely incoming president of China] is reserved—not in the sense that he will not talk to you, but in the sense that he will not betray his likes and dislikes. There is always a pleasant smile on his face, whether or not you have said something that annoyed him. He has iron in his soul, more than Hu Jintao, who ascended the ranks without experiencing the trials and tribulations that Xi endured.

5. China is not going to become a liberal democracy; if it did, it would collapse. Of that, I am quite sure, and the Chinese intelligentsia also understands that. If you believe that there is going to be a revolution of some sort in China for democracy, you are wrong. Where are the students of Tiananmen now? They are irrelevant.

6. I understood Deng Xiaoping when he said: if 200,000 students have to be shot, shoot them, because the alternative is China in chaos for another 100 years. . . . Deng understood, and he released it stage by stage. Without Deng, China would have imploded.

7. The U.S. is going through a bumpy patch with its debt and deficits, but I have no doubt that America will not be reduced to second-rate status. Historically, the U.S. has demonstrated a great capacity for renewal and revival. America's strengths include no grooved thinking, but rather, an ability to range widely, imaginatively, and pragmatically; a diversity of centers of excellence that compete in inventing and embracing new ideas and new technologies; a society that attracts talent from around the world and assimilates them comfortably as Americans; and a language that is the equivalent of an open system that is clearly the lingua franca of the leaders in science, technology, invention, business, education, diplomacy, and those who rise to the top of their own societies around the world.

8. Presidents do not get reelected if they give a hard dose of medicine to their people. So, there is a tendency to procrastinate, to postpone unpopular policies in order to win elections. So problems such as budget deficits, debt, and high unemployment have been carried forward from one administration to the next.

9. The baiting of China by American human rights groups, and the threatening of loss of most-favored-nation status and other sanctions by the U.S. Congress and administration for violations of human rights and missile technology transfers . . . ignore differences of culture, values, and history, and subordinate the strategic considerations of China-U.S. relations to an American domestic agenda. Such a haphazard approach risks turning

China into a long-term adversary of the U.S. Less sensitivity and more understanding of the cultural realities of China can make for a less confrontational relationship.

10. Americans seem to think that Asia is like a movie and that you can freeze developments out here whenever the U.S. becomes intensely involved elsewhere in the world. It does not work like that. If the United States wants to substantially affect the strategic evolution of Asia, it cannot come and go.

11. India has wasted decades in state planning and controls that have bogged it down in bureaucracy and corruption. A decentralized system would have allowed more centers like Bangalore and Bombay to grow and prosper. . . . The caste system has been the enemy of meritocracy. . . . India is a nation of unfulfilled greatness. Its potential has lain fallow, underused.

12. There are limitations in the Indian constitutional system and the Indian political system that prevent it from going at high speed. . . . Whatever the political leadership may want to do, it must go through a very complex system at the center, and then even a more complex system in the various states. . . . Indians will go at a tempo which is decided by their constitution, by their ethnic mix, by their voting patterns, and the resulting coalition governments, which makes for very difficult decision-making.

13. Islam has not been a problem. However, contemporary radical Islam, or Islamism, is a problem. Oil without Islamism can be a problem, but Islamism *plus* oil becomes a volatile mix. Islamism *plus* oil *plus* weapons of mass destruction equals a threat. . . . A nuclear-capable Iran will significantly alter the geopolitical balance. . . . A conflict in the Middle East over the bomb that Iran is developing . . . would have a catastrophic impact on markets. Iran's nuclear program is the challenge that the world is most likely to bungle. . . . If Iran gets the bomb, Saudi Arabia will buy the bomb from Pakistan, the Egyptians will buy the bomb from someone, and then you have a nuclearized Middle East. Then it is only a matter of time before there is a nuclear explosion in the region.

14. The day [Mikhail] Gorbachev said to the masses in Moscow: do not be afraid of the KGB, I took a deep breath. This man is a real genius, I said. . . . He is sitting on top of a terror machine that holds the damn pile together, and he says: do not be afraid. He must have a tremendous formula to democratize. Until I met him, and I found him completely bewildered by what was happening around him. He had jumped into the deep end of the pool without learning how to swim.

15. The Russian population is declining. It is not clear why, but alcoholism plays a role; so do pessimism, a declining fertility rate, and a declining life expectancy. . . . Siberia and Vladivostok are filling up with more and more Chinese. The lands on the bend

of the Amur River will be repopulated by Chinese. Russians may suddenly decide that the future is worth living and bring more children into the world to reverse this demographic trend, but I do not see that shift occurring in the near future.

16. There are no historical precedents on how to maintain peace and stability and to ensure cooperation in a world of 160 nation-states. And the age of instant communications and swift transportation, with technology growing exponentially, makes this problem very complex. In one interdependent, interrelated world, the decline in the relative dominance of the leaders of the two blocs increases the likelihood of a multipolar world, and with it the difficulties of multilateral cooperation.

17. There is no viable alternative to global integration. Protectionism disguised as regionalism will sooner or later lead to conflicts and wars between the regional blocs as they compete for advantage in non-bloc areas, like the oil countries of the Gulf. Globalism is the only answer that is fair, acceptable, and will uphold world peace.

18. They [the BRICs] are different countries on different continents that happen to be growing faster than other combinations of countries on those continents, so somebody said: why not bring them all together and make them into a global force? . . . The Chinese and Indians do not share the same dreams.

19. Westerners have abandoned an ethical basis for society, believing that all problems are solvable by a good government. . . . In the West, especially after World War II, the government came to be seen as so successful that it could fulfill all the obligations that in less modern societies are fulfilled by the family. . . . In the East, we start with self-reliance. In the West today, it is the opposite. The government says give me a popular mandate and I will solve all society's problems.

20. In any given society, of the 1,000 babies born, there are so many percent near-geniuses, so many percent average, so many percent morons. . . . It is the near-geniuses and the above-average who ultimately decide the shape of things to come. . . . We want an equal society. We want to give everybody equal opportunities. But, in the back of our minds, we never deceive ourselves that two human beings are ever equal in their stamina, in their drive, in their dedication, in their innate ability.

21. I do not want to be remembered as a statesman. First of all, I do not classify myself as a statesman. I put myself down as determined, consistent, persistent. I set out to do something. I keep on chasing it until it succeeds. That is all. . . . Anybody who thinks he is a statesman needs to see a psychiatrist.

Notes

CHAPTER 1

1. Lee Kuan Yew, interview with Graham Allison and Robert D. Blackwill, May 11, 2011.
2. Lee Kuan Yew, "China: An Economic Giant?" speech given at the Fortune Global Forum, Shanghai, September 29, 1999.
3. Lee Kuan Yew, interview with Arnaud de Borchgrave, United Press International, February 8, 2008.
4. Lee Kuan Yew, "China's Growing Might and the Consequences," *Forbes*, March 28, 2011.
5. Lee Kuan Yew, speech given at the U.S.-ASEAN Business Council's 25th Anniversary Gala Dinner, Washington, D.C., October 27, 2009.
6. Lee Kuan Yew, interview with Graham Allison and Robert D. Blackwill, May 11, 2011.
7. Edward Cody, "China Not a U.S. Rival, Beijing Official Says; Opposition Expressed to Power Politics in Asia," *Washington Post*, January 18, 1997.

8. Lee Kuan Yew, "Asia and the World in the 21st Century," speech given at the 21st Century Forum, Beijing, September 4, 1996.

9. Han Fook Kwang, Zuraidah Ibrahim, Chua Mui Hoong, Lydia Lim, Ignatius Low, Rachel Lin, and Robin Chan, *Lee Kuan Yew: Hard Truths to Keep Singapore Going* (Singapore: Straits Times, 2011), p. 331.

10. Lee Kuan Yew, speech given at the U.S.-ASEAN Business Council's 25th Anniversary Gala Dinner.

11. Deputy Secretary Steinberg's May 30, 2009, conversation with Singapore Minister Mentor Lee Kuan Yew, classified cable from Daniel L. Shields, former U.S. deputy chief of mission to the Singapore Embassy, June 4, 2009.

12. Lee Kuan Yew, "It's Stupid to Be Afraid," interview with *Der Spiegel*, August 8, 2005.

13. Lee Kuan Yew, "Contest for Influence in the Asia-Pacific Region," *Forbes*, June 18, 2007.

14. Lee Kuan Yew, interview with Michael Elliott, Zoher Abdoolcarim, and Simon Elegant, *Time*, December 12, 2005.

15. Lee Kuan Yew on Burma's "stupid" generals and the "gambler" Chen Shuibian, classified cable from Patricia L. Herbold, former U.S. ambassador to Singapore, October 17, 2009.

16. Lee Kuan Yew, interview with Graham Allison and Robert D. Blackwill, December 2, 2011.

17. Erik Eckholm and Joseph Kahn, "Asia Worries about Growth of China's Economic Power," *New York Times*, November 24, 2002.

18. Lee Kuan Yew, interview with Graham Allison and Robert D. Blackwill, May 11, 2011.

19. Ibid.

20. Lee Kuan Yew, interview with Graham Allison and Robert D. Blackwill, December 2, 2011.

21. Lee Kuan Yew, speech given at the Lincoln Award Medal Ceremony, Washington, D.C., October 18, 2011.

22. William Safire, "Danger: Chinese Tinderbox," *New York Times*, February 22, 1999.

23. Fareed Zakaria, "Culture Is Destiny: A Conversation with Lee Kuan Yew," *Foreign Affairs*, Vol. 73, No. 2 (March/April 1994), p. 123.

24. Lee Kuan Yew, interview with Charlie Rose, March 28, 2011.

25. Tom Plate, *Conversations with Lee Kuan Yew: Citizen Singapore: How to Build a Nation* (Singapore: Marshall Cavendish, 2010), p. 113.

26. Ibid., p. 72.

27. Lee Kuan Yew, interview with Charlie Rose, October 22, 2009.

28. Lee Kuan Yew, interview with Leonard M. Apcar, Wayne Arnold, and Seth Mydans, *International Herald Tribune*, August 29, 2007.

29. Lee Kuan Yew, interview with Graham Allison and Robert D. Blackwill, May 11, 2011.

30. Lee Kuan Yew, speech given at the Lincoln Award Medal Ceremony.

31. Lee Kuan Yew, interview with Graham Allison and Robert D. Blackwill, May 11, 2011.

32. Ibid.

33. Kwang et al., *Lee Kuan Yew: Hard Truths to Keep Singapore Going*, pp. 321–322.

34. Ibid., p. 302.

35. Lee Kuan Yew, "China's Rise: A Shift in Global Influence," *Forbes*, December 20, 2010.

36. Question and answer session with Lee Kuan Yew at the International Institute for Strategic Studies, London, September 23, 2008.

37. Lee Kuan Yew, speech given at the Lincoln Award Medal Ceremony.

38. Lee Kuan Yew, speech given at the World Chinese Entrepreneurs Convention, Singapore, August 10, 1991.

39. Lee Kuan Yew, interview with the Public Broadcasting Service, May 5, 2001.

40. Lee Kuan Yew, "News from a Time Capsule," *Economist*, September 11, 1993.

41. Lee Kuan Yew, "The Fundamentals of Singapore's Foreign Policy: Then and Now," S. Rajaratnam Lecture, Singapore, April 9, 2009.

42. "Transcript of Senior Minister's News Conference with the Local Media in Beijing, 12 June 2001," June 15, 2001.

43. Lee Kuan Yew, interview with Tom Plate and Jeffrey Cole, *AsiaMedia*, October 9, 2007.

44. Lee Kuan Yew, "Asia and the World in the 21st Century."

45. Lee Kuan Yew, interview with Graham Allison and Robert D. Blackwill, March 28, 2012.

46. Simon Elegant, "China's Nelson Mandela," *Time*, November 19, 2007.

CHAPTER 2

1. Lee Kuan Yew, interview with Graham Allison and Robert D. Blackwill, May 11, 2011.

2. Lee Kuan Yew, speech given at the Lincoln Award Medal Ceremony, Washington, D.C., October 18, 2011.

3. Lee Kuan Yew, speech given at the U.S.-ASEAN Business Council's 25th Anniversary Gala Dinner, Washington, D.C., October 27, 2009; and Lee Kuan Yew, "The World after Iraq," speech given at the Thammasat Business School International Forum, Bangkok, December 16, 2003.

4. Lee Kuan Yew, "Challenges of Small City-States in a Globalized World," speech given at the inauguration of the Investment Corporation of Dubai, Dubai, March 1, 2008; and Lee Kuan Yew, "The Fundamentals of Singapore's Foreign Policy: Then and Now," S. Rajaratnam Lecture, Singapore, April 9, 2009.

5. Lee Kuan Yew, "The World after 9/11," speech given at the Munich Economic Summit, Munich, June 7, 2002.

6. Lee Kuan Yew, speech given at the Tanjong Pagar 39th National Day Celebration Dinner, Singapore, August 20, 2004.

7. Lee Kuan Yew, interview with Tom Plate and Jeffrey Cole, *AsiaMedia*, October 9, 2007.

8. Lee Kuan Yew, interview with Michael Elliott, Zoher Abdoolcarim, and Simon Elegant, *Time*, December 12, 2005.

9. Lee Kuan Yew, speech given at the Forbes Global CEO Conference Gala Dinner, Singapore, September 19, 2001.

10. Lee Kuan Yew, "An Entrepreneurial Culture for Singapore," Ho Rih Hwa Leadership in Asia Public Lecture, Singapore, February 5, 2002.

11. Han Fook Kwang, Zuraidah Ibrahim, Chua Mui Hoong, Lydia Lim, Ignatius Low, Rachel Lin, and Robin Chan, *Lee Kuan Yew: Hard Truths to Keep Singapore Going* (Singapore: Straits Times, 2011), pp. 150–151.

12. Lee Kuan Yew, interview with Peter Day, BBC, May 13, 2000.

13. Lee Kuan Yew, "Eastern and Western Cultures and Modernization," speech given at the China Scientists Forum on Humanities, Beijing, April 21, 2004.

14. Patrick Barta and Robert Thomson, "Singapore's 'Mentor' Seeks a Sturdy U.S.," *Wall Street Journal*, April 27, 2011; Kwan Weng Kin, "Only U.S. Can Balance China," *Straits Times*, May 27, 2011; and Yoichi Funabashi, "Maintaining Balance of Power in Asia Requires U.S. Engagement," *Asahi Shimbun*, May 15, 2010.

15. Lee Kuan Yew, "What Has the Future in Store for Your Generation?" speech given at the Nanyang Auditorium, Singapore, February 18, 2003.

16. Lee Kuan Yew, "Changes in the Wind," *Forbes*, October 19, 2009.

17. Lee Kuan Yew, "Peace and Progress in East Asia," speech given at a joint meeting of Congress, Washington, D.C., October 9, 1985.

18. Lee Kuan Yew, *From Third World to First: The Singapore Story, 1965–2000* (New York: HarperCollins, 2000), pp. 498, 500.

19. Chuang Peck Ming, "LKY Cautions against Two-Party Political System," *Business Times*, September 15, 2011.

20. Barta and Thomson, "Singapore's 'Mentor' Seeks a Sturdy U.S."

21. Lee Kuan Yew, interview with Graham Allison and Robert D. Blackwill, December 2, 2011.

22. Lee Kuan Yew, "East Asia in the New Era: The Prospects of Cooperation," speech given at the Harvard Fairbank Center Conference, New York, May 11, 1992.

23. Tom Plate, *Conversations with Lee Kuan Yew: Citizen Singapore: How to Build a Nation* (Singapore: Marshall Cavendish, 2010), p. 91.

24. Lee Kuan Yew, "For Third World Leaders: Hope or Despair?" Collins Family International Fellowship Lecture, Cambridge, Massachusetts, October 17, 2000.

25. Lee Kuan Yew, speech given at the Philippine Business Conference, Manila, November 18, 1992.

26. Ibid.

27. Lee Kuan Yew, interview with Graham Allison and Robert D. Blackwill, December 2, 2011.

28. "The View from Singapore," *Time*, July 25, 1969.

29. Fareed Zakaria, "Culture Is Destiny: A Conversation with Lee Kuan Yew," *Foreign Affairs*, Vol. 73, No. 2 (March/April 1994), pp. 111–114.

30. Nathan Gardels, "City of the Future: What America Can Learn from Post-Liberal Singapore," *Washington Post*, February 11, 1996.

31. Lee Kuan Yew, speech given at the Create 21 Asahi Forum, Tokyo, November 20, 1992.

32. "Li vs. Lee," *Wall Street Journal*, August 24, 2004.

33. Lee Kuan Yew, "Exciting Times Ahead," speech given at the Tanjong Pagar GRC National Day Dinner, Singapore, August 12, 1995.

34. Kwang et al., *Lee Kuan Yew: Hard Truths to Keep Singapore Going*, p. 56; and Lee Kuan Yew, interview with Graham Allison and Robert D. Blackwill, December 2, 2011.

35. Lee Kuan Yew, interview with Tom Plate and Jeffrey Cole.

36. Kwang et al., *Lee Kuan Yew: Hard Truths to Keep Singapore Going*, p. 434.

37. Lee Kuan Yew, letter to Singapore's media, January 18, 2012.

38. Han Fook Kwang, Warren Fernandez, and Sumiko Tan, *Lee Kuan Yew: The Man and His Ideas* (Singapore: Straits Times, 1998), p. 134.

39. Lee Kuan Yew, "How Much Is a Good Minister Worth?" speech given at a debate in the Singaporean parliament on ministerial salaries, Singapore, November 1, 1994.

40. Michael D. Barr, *Lee Kuan Yew: The Beliefs behind the Man* (Washington, D.C.: Georgetown University Press, 2000), p. 212.

41. Lee Kuan Yew, "New Bearings in Our Education System," speech given to principals of schools in Singapore, Singapore, August 29, 1966.

42. Lee Kuan Yew, speech given at a "Dinner for the Establishment," Singapore, September 25, 1984.

43. Faris Mokhtar, "Foreign Talent Allows S'pore to Punch above Its Weight," Yahoo, July 22, 2011.

44. Secretary of Labor Chao meets Singapore Lee Kuan Yew, Singapore Minister

Mentor, August 29, 2008, classified cable from Patricia L. Herbold, former U.S. ambassador to Singapore, September 18, 2008.

45. Lee Kuan Yew, "Will Singapore Be Another Slow-Growing Developed Nation?" speech given at the Nanyang Technological University, Singapore, March 14, 1996.

46. Lee Kuan Yew, speech given at the Singapore American School's 50th Anniversary Celebration, Singapore, April 11, 2006.

47. Question and answer session with Lee Kuan Yew at the APEC CEO Summit, Singapore, November 13, 2009.

48. Lee Kuan Yew, interview with Charlie Rose, October 22, 2009.

49. Lee Kuan Yew, speech given at the U.S.-ASEAN Business Council's 25th Anniversary Gala Dinner.

50. Lee Kuan Yew, interview with Charlie Rose.

51. Christopher S. Bond and Lewis M. Simons, *The Next Front: Southeast Asia and the Road to Global Peace with Islam* (New York: John Wiley and Sons, 2009), p. 223.

CHAPTER 3

1. Lee Kuan Yew, interview with Graham Allison and Robert D. Blackwill, December 2, 2011.

2. Lee Kuan Yew, interview with Charlie Rose, March 28, 2011.

3. Lee Kuan Yew, speech given at the U.S.-ASEAN Business Council's 25th Anniversary Gala Dinner, Washington, D.C., October 27, 2009.

4. Lee Kuan Yew, speech given at the International Institute for Strategic Studies Conference, Singapore, September 12, 1997.

5. Lee Kuan Yew, "Battle for Preeminence," *Forbes*, October 11, 2010; and Lee Kuan Yew, speech given at the Fortune 500 Forum, Boston, October 23, 1997.

6. Lee Kuan Yew, interview with Graham Allison and Robert D. Blackwill, December 2, 2011.

7. Lee Kuan Yew, speech given at the International Institute for Strategic Studies Conference.

8. Lee Kuan Yew, speech given at the *Asahi Shimbun* Symposium, Tokyo, May 9, 1991.

9. Patrick Barta and Robert Thomson, "Singapore's 'Mentor' Seeks a Sturdy U.S.," *Wall Street Journal*, April 27, 2011.

10. P. Parameswaran, "U.S. Must Engage Asia to Maintain Global Power: Lee," Agence France-Presse, October 27, 2009.

11. Lee Kuan Yew, "East Asia in the New Era: The Prospects of Cooperation," speech given at the Harvard Fairbank Center Conference, New York, May 11, 1992.

12. Lee Kuan Yew, "Japan's Role in the 21st Century," speech given at the Asahi Forum, Tokyo, November 17, 1994.

13. Lee Kuan Yew, "East Asia in the New Era: The Prospects of Cooperation."

14. Lee Kuan Yew, "America and Asia," speech given at the Architect of the New Century Award Ceremony, Washington, D.C., November 11, 1996.

15. Nathan Gardels, "The East Asian Way—with Air Conditioning," *New Perspectives Quarterly*, Vol. 26, No. 4 (Fall 2009), p. 116.

16. Lee Kuan Yew, speech given at the Lincoln Award Medal Ceremony, Washington, D.C., October 18, 2011.

17. Summary of a conversation between Lee Kuan Yew and John Thornton at the FutureChina Global Forum, Singapore, July 11, 2011.

18. Nicholas D. Kristof, "The Rise of China," *Foreign Affairs*, Vol. 72, No. 5 (November/December 1993), p. 74.

19. Lee Kuan Yew, "China's Rise: A Shift in Global Influence," *Forbes*, December 20, 2010.

20. Lee Kuan Yew, interview with Graham Allison and Robert D. Blackwill, December 2, 2011.

21. Lee Kuan Yew, speech given at the Amex Bank Review Awards Global Forum, Singapore, November 15, 1993.

22. Lee Kuan Yew, speech given at the Create 21 Asahi Symposium, Osaka, November 19, 1996.

23. Lee Kuan Yew, "The Rise of East Asia in the World Economy: Geopolitical and Geoeconomic Implications," speech given at the Asia Society Conference, Singapore, May 19, 1994.

24. Lee Kuan Yew, speech given at the Create 21 Asahi Symposium.

25. Lee Kuan Yew, interview with Graham Allison and Robert D. Blackwill, May 11, 2011.

26. Ibid.

27. Lee Kuan Yew, "The Rise of East Asia in the World Economy."

28. Lee Kuan Yew, speech given at the Create 21 Asahi Symposium.

29. Lee Kuan Yew, "America and Asia."

30. Lee Kuan Yew, "The Dawn of the Pacific Century," speech given at the Pacific Rim Forum, San Diego, California, May 13, 1992.

31. Lee Kuan Yew, "The Rise of East Asia: Challenges and Opportunities," speech given at the World Economic Forum Summit, Singapore, September 20, 1995.

32. "U.S. Holds Key to Asian Security—Lee," Reuters, May 16, 1993.

33. Question and answer session with Lee Kuan Yew at the Lee Kuan Yew

School of Public Policy's 5th Anniversary Gala Dinner, Singapore, September 2, 2009.

34. Lee Kuan Yew, "Shanghai's Role in China's Renaissance," speech given at the 2005 Shanghai Forum, Shanghai, May 17, 2005.

35. Lee Kuan Yew, interview with Graham Allison and Robert D. Blackwill, May 11, 2011.

CHAPTER 4

1. Lee Kuan Yew, *From Third World to First: The Singapore Story, 1965–2000* (New York: HarperCollins, 2000), p. 405.

2. Ibid., p. 412.

3. Lee Kuan Yew, speech given at the launch of Narayana Murthy's *A Better India: A Better World*, Singapore, May 11, 2009.

4. Sunanda K. Datta-Ray, *Looking East to Look West: Lee Kuan Yew's Mission India* (Singapore: ISEAS, 2009), p. 153.

5. Lee Kuan Yew, "Managing Globalization: Lessons from India and China," speech given at the official opening of the Lee Kuan Yew School of Public Policy, Singapore, April 4, 2005.

6. Lee Kuan Yew, speech given at the launch of Narayana Murthy's *A Better India: A Better World*.

7. Lee Kuan Yew, interview with Graham Allison and Robert D. Blackwill, December 2, 2011.

8. Han Fook Kwang, Zuraidah Ibrahim, Chua Mui Hoong, Lydia Lim, Ignatius Low, Rachel Lin, and Robin Chan, *Lee Kuan Yew: Hard Truths to Keep Singapore Going* (Singapore: Straits Times, 2011), p. 50.

9. Tom Plate, *Conversations with Lee Kuan Yew: Citizen Singapore: How to Build a Nation* (Singapore: Marshall Cavendish, 2010), p. 102.

10. Elgin Toh, "Mr. Lee Optimistic over China's Development; He Predicts Next Leader Will Seek to Take Country to Higher Level," *Straits Times*, July 12, 2011.

11. Lee Kuan Yew, "India in an Asian Renaissance," 37th Jawaharlal Nehru Lecture, New Delhi, November 21, 2005.

12. Lee Kuan Yew, "Managing Globalization."

13. Lee Kuan Yew, "India in an Asian Renaissance."

14. Lee Kuan Yew, "Managing Globalization."

15. Rasheeda Bhagat, "Lee's Recipe for India," *Hindu Business Line*, October 14, 2008.

16. Datta-Ray, *Looking East to Look West*, pp. 223–224.

17. Ibid., p. 279.

18. Ravi Velloor, "India's Economy on a Roll, but Mind the Humps," *Straits Times*, November 10, 2007.

19. Lee Kuan Yew, "Managing Globalization."

20. Ravi Velloor, "India Will Play Independent Role: MM Lee," *Straits Times*, November 5, 2007.

21. "India, China Unlikely to Resolve Border Dispute: Lee Kuan Yew," Press Trust of India, December 16, 2009.

22. Lee Kuan Yew, "India in an Asian Renaissance."

23. Ibid.

24. Lee Kuan Yew, "Managing Globalization."

25. "Lee Kuan Yew Suggests Strategy for India to Grow beyond Current Rate of Growth," Xinhua, December 17, 2009.

26. Datta-Ray, *Looking East to Look West*, pp. 298–299.

27. Lee Kuan Yew, "India in an Asian Renaissance."

28. Lee Kuan Yew, interview with the Public Broadcasting Service, May 5, 2001.

29. Lee Kuan Yew, "A Tryst with Destiny," speech given at a joint meeting of the Associated Chambers of Commerce and Industry of India, the Federation of Indian Chambers of Commerce and Industry, and the Federation of Indian Industries, New Delhi, January 5, 1996.

30. Ibid.

31. Kwang et al., *Lee Kuan Yew*, pp. 284–285.

32. Lee Kuan Yew, "Managing Globalization."

33. Kwang et al., *Lee Kuan Yew*, p. 318.

34. Ibid.

35. Lee Kuan Yew, interview with Leonard M. Apcar, Wayne Arnold, and Seth Mydans, *International Herald Tribune*, August 29, 2007.

36. Lee Kuan Yew, "India's Peaceful Rise," *Forbes*, December 24, 2007.

37. P. S. Suryanarayana, "China, India Not Basically Adversaries: Lee Kuan Yew," *Hindu*, July 24, 2011.

38. Lee Kuan Yew, interview with Charlie Rose, March 28, 2011.

39. Question and answer session with Lee Kuan Yew at the International Institute for Strategic Studies, London, September 23, 2008.

40. Lee Kuan Yew, interview with Graham Allison and Robert D. Blackwill.

41. Lee Kuan Yew, "A Tryst with Destiny."

42. Lee Kuan Yew, "India in an Asian Renaissance."

43. Lee Kuan Yew, "Managing Globalization."

44. Lee Kuan Yew, "India in an Asian Renaissance."

45. Datta-Ray, *Looking East to Look West*, p. 7.

46. Kripa Sridharan, "The Evolution and Growth of India-Singapore Relations," in Yong Mun Cheong and V. V. Bhanoji Rao, eds., *Singapore-India Relations: A Primer* (Singapore: Singapore University Press, 1995), p. 23.

47. Datta-Ray, *Looking East to Look West*, p. 81.

48. Plate, *Conversations with Lee Kuan Yew*, pp. 105–106.

49. Lee Kuan Yew, interview with Graham Allison and Robert D. Blackwill.

50. Kwang et al., *Lee Kuan Yew*, p. 315.

51. Lee Kuan Yew, interview with Graham Allison and Robert D. Blackwill.

52. Velloor, "India Will Play Independent Role."

CHAPTER 5

1. Lee Kuan Yew, "Uncertainties Abound," speech given at the Tanjong Pagar 37th National Day Celebration Dinner, Singapore, August 16, 2002.

2. Han Fook Kwang, Zuraidah Ibrahim, Chua Mui Hoong, Lydia Lim, Ignatius Low, Rachel Lin, and Robin Chan, *Lee Kuan Yew: Hard Truths to Keep Singapore Going* (Singapore: Straits Times, 2011), p. 239.

3. Fareed Zakaria, "We Need to Get the Queen Bees," *Newsweek*, December 1, 2003.

4. Lee Kuan Yew, "Homegrown Islamic Terrorists," *Forbes*, October 17, 2005.

5. Lee Kuan Yew, "Oil and Islamism," *Forbes*, March 13, 2006 (emphasis in original).

6. Senator Baucus's meeting with Lee Kuan Yew, classified cable from Patricia L. Herbold, former U.S. ambassador to Singapore, January 17, 2006.

7. Lee Kuan Yew, "The East Asian Strategic Balance after 9/11," speech given at the 1st International Institute for Strategic Studies Asia Security Conference, Singapore, May 31, 2002.

8. Lee Kuan Yew, "After Iraq," speech given at the 2nd International Institute for Strategic Studies Asia Security Conference, Singapore, May 30, 2003.

9. Lee Kuan Yew, "The East Asian Strategic Balance after 9/11."

10. Lee Kuan Yew, "What Went Wrong?" interview with Michael Vatikiotis, *Far Eastern Economic Review*, December 2002.

11. Lee Kuan Yew, interview with Charlie Rose, September 24, 2004.

12. Christopher S. Bond and Lewis M. Simons, *The Next Front: Southeast Asia and the Road to Global Peace with Islam* (New York: John Wiley and Sons, 2009), p. 223.

13. Tom Plate, *Conversations with Lee Kuan Yew: Citizen Singapore: How to Build a Nation* (Singapore: Marshall Cavendish, 2010), pp. 117–118.

14. Kwang et al., *Lee Kuan Yew*, pp. 228, 230.

15. Lee Kuan Yew, "Oil and Islamism."

16. Lee Kuan Yew, interview with Charlie Rose.

17. Lee Kuan Yew, "Terrorism," *Forbes*, December 26, 2005.

18. Lee Kuan Yew, speech given at the Singaporean parliament on the proposal to develop integrated resorts, Singapore, April 19, 2005.

19. Lee Kuan Yew, interview with Arnaud de Borchgrave, United Press International, February 8, 2008.

20. Lee Kuan Yew, "What Went Wrong?"

21. Lee Kuan Yew, speech given at the Tanjong Pagar 40th National Day Celebration Dinner, Singapore, August 12, 2005.

22. Lee Kuan Yew, interview with Graham Allison and Robert D. Blackwill, December 2, 2011.

23. Plate, *Conversations with Lee Kuan Yew*, p. 120.

24. Lee Kuan Yew, "The Cost of Retreat in Iraq," *Washington Post*, March 8, 2008.

25. Lee Kuan Yew, "The United States, Iraq, and the War on Terror: A Singa-

porean Perspective," *Foreign Affairs*, Vol. 86, No. 1 (January/February 2007), p. 3.

26. Lee Kuan Yew, "Islam and Democracy in Southeast Asia," *Forbes*, July 26, 2004.

27. Zakaria, "We Need to Get the Queen Bees."

28. Lee Kuan Yew, "Can We Ever Understand Muslim Terrorists?" *Forbes*, October 13, 2003.

29. Press statement by Yeong Yoon Ying on behalf of Lee Kuan Yew, September 5, 2011.

30. Lee Kuan Yew, "What Has the Future in Store for Your Generation?" speech given at the Nanyang Auditorium, Singapore, February 18, 2003.

31. Lee Kuan Yew, "The World after Iraq," speech given at the Thammasat Business School International Forum, Bangkok, December 16, 2003.

32. "Lee Kuan Yew Gives Warning to Islamic Moderates," Agence France-Presse, March 28, 2004.

33. Lee Kuan Yew, "The East Asian Strategic Balance after 9/11."

34. Lee Kuan Yew, "Homegrown Islamic Terrorists," *Forbes*, October 17, 2005.

35. Lee, "The United States, Iraq, and the War on Terror," pp. 3–4.

36. Lee Kuan Yew, interview with Michael Elliott, Zoher Abdoolcarim, and Simon Elegant, *Time*, December 12, 2005.

37. Lee Kuan Yew, "The East Asian Strategic Balance after 9/11."

38. "Islamic Terrorism to Remain: Lee Kuan Yew," *People's Daily*, October 14, 2004.

39. Visit by Senator Clinton to Singapore (July 5–7), classified cable from Frank L. Lavin, former U.S. ambassador to Singapore, July 6, 2005.

40. Zakaria, "We Need to Get the Queen Bees."

41. Lee Kuan Yew, interview with Arnaud de Borchgrave.

CHAPTER 6

1. Han Fook Kwang, Zuraidah Ibrahim, Chua Mui Hoong, Lydia Lim, Ignatius Low, Rachel Lin, and Robin Chan, *Lee Kuan Yew: Hard Truths to Keep Singapore Going* (Singapore: Straits Times, 2011), p. 292.

2. Ibid., pp. 156–157.

3. Fareed Zakaria, "Culture Is Destiny: A Conversation with Lee Kuan Yew," *Foreign Affairs*, Vol. 73, No. 2 (March/April 1994), p. 120 (emphasis in the original).

4. Lee Kuan Yew, "For Third World Leaders: Hope or Despair?" Collins Family International Fellowship Lecture, Cambridge, Massachusetts, October 17, 2000.

5. Lee Kuan Yew, speech given at the National Day rally at the Singapore Conference Hall, Singapore, August 18, 1985.

6. Lee Kuan Yew, "Laissez-Faire Procreation," *Foreign Policy*, August 30, 2005.

7. Lee Kuan Yew, "Global Realignment: An Interpretation of Asia's New Dynamism," speech given at the Global Strategies Conference, Singapore, June 6, 1990.

8. Lee Kuan Yew, "Attributes for Success," speech given at the 1999 Enterprise 50 Gala Dinner and Award Ceremony, Singapore, November 25, 1999.

9. Lee Kuan Yew, "Eastern and Western Cultures and Modernization," speech given at the China Scientists Forum on Humanities, Beijing, April 21, 2004.

10. Lee Kuan Yew, speech given at the Singapore International Chamber of Commerce Celebration Dinner, Singapore, November 15, 2000.

11. Lee Kuan Yew, speech given at the Millennium Law Conference Gala Dinner, Singapore, April 11, 2000.

12. Lee Kuan Yew, speech given at the Singapore TechVenture 2000 Conference, San Francisco, California, March 9, 2000.

13. Lee Kuan Yew, "Asia, America, and Europe in the Next Millennium: Towards Economic Complementarity and Convergence," speech given at the ABN-AMRO Symposium, Amsterdam, June 6, 1997 (emphasis in the original).

14. Lee Kuan Yew, "Uncertainties Abound," speech given at the Tanjong Pagar 37th National Day Celebration Dinner, Singapore, August 16, 2002.

15. Lee Kuan Yew, speech given at the Tanjong Pagar 34th National Day Celebration, Singapore, August 14, 1999.

16. Lee Kuan Yew, May Day message, May 1, 1984.

17. Kwang et al., *Lee Kuan Yew*, pp. 173–174.

18. Lee Kuan Yew, "Managing Globalization: Lessons from China and India," speech given at the official opening of the Lee Kuan Yew School of Public Policy, Singapore, April 4, 2005.

19. Lee Kuan Yew, "Singapore: A 21st-Century Economy," speech given at the Barcelona Chamber of Commerce, Industry, and Shipping, Barcelona, September 14, 2005.

20. Kevin Hamlin, "Remaking Singapore," *Institutional Investor*, May 2002.

21. Lee Kuan Yew, "Productivity: Time for Action," speech given at the inauguration of Productivity Month 1983 at the Singapore Conference Hall, Singapore, November 1, 1983.

22. Zakaria, "Culture Is Destiny," pp. 114–115.

23. Lee Kuan Yew, speech given at the Chinese New Year Reception, Singapore, February 15, 1984.

24. Lee Kuan Yew, "Productivity: Every Individual Makes the Difference," speech given at the inauguration of the 1999 Productivity Campaign, Singapore, April 9, 1999.

25. Lee Kuan Yew, speech given at the launch of the English Language Institute of Singapore, Singapore, September 6, 2011.

C H A P T E R   7

1. Lee Kuan Yew, interview with Graham Allison and Robert D. Blackwill, March 28, 2012.

2. Ibid.

3. Lee Kuan Yew, interview with Charlie Rose, October 22, 2009.

4. Lee Kuan Yew, interview with Graham Allison and Robert D. Blackwill.

5. Ibid.

6. Lee Kuan Yew, speech given at the U.S.-ASEAN Business Council's 25th Anniversary Gala Dinner, Washington, D.C., October 27, 2009.

7. Lee Kuan Yew, "The Fundamentals of Singapore's Foreign Policy: Then and Now," S. Rajaratnam Lecture, Singapore, April 9, 2009.

8. Question and answer session with Lee Kuan Yew at the Lee Kuan Yew School of Public Policy's 5th Anniversary Gala Dinner, Singapore, September 2, 2009.

9. Question and answer session with Lee Kuan Yew at the APEC CEO Summit, Singapore, November 13, 2009.

10. Lee Kuan Yew, "2009 Will Test the Character of Singaporeans," speech given at the Tanjong Pagar Chinese New Year Dinner, Singapore, February 6, 2009.

11. Lee Kuan Yew, "Changes in the Wind," *Forbes*, October 19, 2009.

12. Lee Kuan Yew, "The World Is Truly a Global Village," *Forbes*, March 26, 2012.

13. Lee Kuan Yew, "How Will Singapore Compete in a Global Economy?"

speech given at Nanyang Technological University, Singapore, February 15, 2000.

14. Lee Kuan Yew, "The Role of Singapore in the Asian Boom," speech given at the International Graduate School of Management, Barcelona, September 13, 2005.

15. Lee Kuan Yew, "More Globalized, More Troubled," *Forbes*, October 15, 2007.

16. Lee Kuan Yew, "What Has the Future in Store for Your Generation?" speech given at the Nanyang Auditorium, Singapore, February 18, 2003.

17. Lee Kuan Yew, speech given at the Tanjong Pagar 42nd National Day Celebration Dinner, Singapore, August 17, 2007.

18. Lee Kuan Yew, speech given at the Commemoration Conference of Confucius's 2,550th Birthday and the 2nd Congress of the International Confucius Association, Beijing, October 7, 1999.

19. Lee Kuan Yew, speech given at the 21st Century Forum on "Economic Globalization—China and Asia," Beijing, June 14, 2000.

20. Lee Kuan Yew, speech given at a meeting of the Commonwealth Heads of Government on "World Political Scene: Global Trends and Prospects," Vancouver, October 13, 1987.

21. Lee Kuan Yew, speech given at the Forbes Global CEO Conference Gala Dinner, Singapore, September 19, 2001.

22. Lee Kuan Yew, speech given at the National Trade Union Congress 40th Anniversary Dinner, Singapore, September 6, 2001.

23. Lee Kuan Yew, "How Will Singapore Compete in a Global Economy?"

24. Lee Kuan Yew, speech given at the Japanese Chamber of Commerce and Industry in Singapore's 30th Anniversary Celebration, Singapore, January 28, 2000.

25. Lee Kuan Yew, "To Roll with Change but Not Abandon Values," *Straits Times*, July 22, 2000.

26. Lee Kuan Yew, speech given at the Asian Strategy and Leadership Institute's "World Ethics and Integrity Forum," Kuala Lumpur, April 28, 2005.

27. Lee Kuan Yew, "The Fundamentals of Singapore's Foreign Policy: Then and Now."

28. Lee Kuan Yew, interview with Leonard M. Apcar, Wayne Arnold, and Seth Mydans, *International Herald Tribune*, August 29, 2007.

29. Lee Kuan Yew, "Economic Order or Disorder after the Cold War?" speech given at the Asahi Forum, Tokyo, October 29, 1993.

CHAPTER 8

1. Lee Kuan Yew, speech given at Tanjong Pagar Community Center's National Day Celebration Dinner, Singapore, August 16, 1984.

2. Radio broadcast of a Lee Kuan Yew speech given on June 5, 1959.

3. Lee Kuan Yew, speech given to Singaporean assemblymen and civil servants, Singapore, November 16, 1959.

4. Lee Kuan Yew, May Day message, May 1, 1962.

5. Radio broadcast of a Lee Kuan Yew speech given on June 2, 1960.

6. Lee Kuan Yew, speech given at the National Recreation Center, Singapore, April 25, 1960.

7. Fareed Zakaria, "Culture Is Destiny: A Conversation with Lee Kuan Yew," *Foreign Affairs*, Vol. 73, No. 2 (March/April 1994), pp. 112–114.

8. Lee Kuan Yew, speech given at Tanjong Pagar's 33rd National Day Celebration, Singapore, August 15, 1998.

9. Tom Plate, *Conversations with Lee Kuan Yew: Citizen Singapore: How to Build a Nation* (Singapore: Marshall Cavendish, 2010), p. 86.

10. Lee Kuan Yew, "Political Leadership in New Societies," speech given at the Singapore Chamber of Commerce, Hong Kong, December 8, 2000.

11. Lee Kuan Yew, speech given at the opening of the second meeting of the Malaysia Solidarity Consultative Committee, Singapore, December 18, 1961.

12. Lee Kuan Yew, speech given at a conference of the People's Action Party, Singapore, November 15, 1982.

13. Lee Kuan Yew, speech given at a "dinner for the Establishment," Singapore, September 25, 1984.

14. Lee Kuan Yew, speech given at the Malaysia Solidarity Day mass rally, Singapore, August 31, 1963.

15. Lee Kuan Yew, speech given at the May Day rally, Singapore, May 1, 1961.

16. Lee Kuan Yew, speech given to the guild of Nanyang University graduates, Singapore, November 6, 1960.

17. Lee Kuan Yew, *From Third World to First: The Singapore Story, 1965–2000* (New York: HarperCollins, 2000), p. 688.

18. Plate, *Conversations with Lee Kuan Yew*, p. 31.

19. Radio broadcast of a press conference with Lee Kuan Yew, November 19, 1961.

20. Lee Kuan Yew, speech given at a luncheon of the Australian parliament, Canberra, October 20, 1976.

21. Question and answer session with Lee Kuan Yew at the Royal Institute for International Affairs, London, May 14, 1962.

22. Han Fook Kwang, Warren Fernandez, and Sumiko Tan, *Lee Kuan Yew: The Man and His Ideas* (Singapore: Straits Times, 1998), p. 127.

23. Ibid., p. 229.

24. Lee Kuan Yew, speech given at the opening of the Civil Service Center, Singapore, August 15, 1959.

25. Lee Kuan Yew, speech given at a seminar on "The Concept of Democracy" at the Political Study Center, Singapore, August 16, 1964.

26. Lee Kuan Yew, speech given at an election rally at City Council, Singapore, December 20, 1957.

27. Lee Kuan Yew, speech given at a rally in Klang, Singapore, April 14, 1964.

28. Lee Kuan Yew, speech given at a dinner of the University of Malaya Student Union, Singapore, November 30, 1961.

29. Lee Kuan Yew, speech given at the swearing-in of the Singaporean Cabinet, Singapore, January 2, 1985.

30. Lee Kuan Yew, speech given on the Preservation of Public Security Ordinance, Singapore, October 8, 1958.

31. Lee Kuan Yew, speech given at a rally in Fullerton Square, Singapore, December 19, 1984.

32. Lee Kuan Yew, speech given at the University of Malaya, Kuala Lumpur, August 28, 1964.

33. Lee Kuan Yew, speech given on the eve of elections in Singapore, April 24, 1964.

34. Zakaria, "Culture Is Destiny," p. 119.

35. Lee Kuan Yew, speech given to Singaporean civil servants at the Political Center, Singapore, June 14, 1962.

36. Richard Lambert, Peter Montagnon, and Will Dawkins, "Veteran Asian Leader Scorns U.S. Policy," *Financial Times*, May 19, 1999.

37. Lee Kuan Yew, speech given to the University of Singapore Law Society Annual Dinner, Singapore, January 18, 1962.

38. Lee Kuan Yew, speech given on the Preservation of Public Security Ordinance, Singapore, October 8, 1958.

39. Lee Kuan Yew, speech given at the Tanjong Pagar National Day Dinner, Singapore, August 13, 1987.

40. Lee Kuan Yew, speech given at the People's Action Party's 45th Anniversary Celebrations, Singapore, November 21, 1999.

41. Lee, *From Third World to First*, p. 106.

42. Lee Kuan Yew, speech given at Tanjong Pagar National Day Celebration, Singapore, August 15, 2010.

CHAPTER 9

1. Han Fook Kwang, Warren Fernandez, and Sumiko Tan, *Lee Kuan Yew: The Man and His Ideas* (Singapore: Straits Times, 1998), p. 194.

2. Lee Kuan Yew, New Year's message, January 1, 1958.

3. Sunanda K. Datta-Ray, *Looking East to Look West: Lee Kuan Yew's Mission India* (Singapore: ISEAS, 2009), p. 177.

4. Lee Kuan Yew, interview with Mark Jacobson, July 6, 2009.

5. Lee Kuan Yew, speech given at the Create 21 Asahi Forum, Tokyo, November 20, 1992.

6. Lee Kuan Yew, "Big and Small Fishes in Asian Waters," speech given at a meeting of the University of Singapore Democratic Socialist Club, Singapore, June 15, 1966.

7. Lee Kuan Yew, speech given at the Tanjong Pagar 41st National Day Celebration Dinner, Singapore, August 18, 2006.

8. Kwang et al., *Lee Kuan Yew: The Man and His Ideas*, p. 175.

9. Lee Kuan Yew, speech given at the University of Singapore Business Administration Society's Inaugural Dinner, Singapore, August 27, 1996.

10. Kwang et al., *Lee Kuan Yew: The Man and His Ideas*, p. 159.

11. Lee Kuan Yew, "U.S.: Opportunities in Asia; Challenges in the Middle East," speech given at Southern Methodist University, Dallas, October 19, 2006.

12. Kwang et al., *Lee Kuan Yew: The Man and His Ideas*, p. 130.

13. Tom Plate, *Conversations with Lee Kuan Yew: Citizen Singapore: How to Build a Nation* (Singapore: Marshall Cavendish, 2010), p. 177.

14. Kwang et al., *Lee Kuan Yew: The Man and His Ideas*, pp. 230, 233.

15. Ibid., p. 245.

16. Plate, *Conversations with Lee Kuan Yew*, pp. 49–50.

17. Kwang et al., *Lee Kuan Yew: The Man and His Ideas*, p. 22.

18. Lee Kuan Yew, speech given on the second reading of "The Constitution of the Republic of Singapore (Amendment) Bill" before the Singaporean parliament, Singapore, July 24, 1984.

19. Lee Kuan Yew, speech given at his 60th birthday dinner, Singapore, September 16, 1983.

20. Radio broadcast of a Lee Kuan Yew speech given on September 4, 1962.

21. Lee Kuan Yew, speech given at the Socialist International Congress, Brussels, September 5, 1964.

22. Lee Kuan Yew, speech given at the launching of the S. H. B. Tug "Tegoh" by H. E. the Yang Di-Pertuan Negara, Singapore, February 27, 1960.

23. Plate, *Conversations with Lee Kuan Yew*, pp. 46–47.

24. Kwang et al., *Lee Kuan Yew: The Man and His Ideas*, p. 109.

25. Ibid., p. 151.

26. Lee Kuan Yew, discussion with five foreign correspondents, recorded at Singapore Broadcasting Corporation, Singapore, October 9, 1984.

27. Lee Kuan Yew, interview with Graham Allison and Robert D. Blackwill, December 2, 2011.

28. Lee Kuan Yew, "History Is Not Made the Way It Is Written," speech given at the People's Action Party's 25th Anniversary Rally, Singapore, January 20, 1980.

29. Lee Kuan Yew, speech given at the Ceremony of Admission to the Degree of Doctor of Laws at Melbourne University, Melbourne, April 21, 1994.

30. Lee Kuan Yew, speech given to Singaporean ministers, ministers of state, and senior civil service officers, Singapore, February 27, 1979.

31. Lee Kuan Yew, "'The Returned Student': Platitudes and Controversy," speech given at the Malayan Forum, London, January 28, 1950.

32. Radio broadcast of a Lee Kuan Yew speech given September 15, 1961.

33. Lee Kuan Yew, speech given at the launch of the Devan Nair Research and Training Endowment Fund, Singapore, September 24, 1966.

34. Lee Kuan Yew, speech given to Singaporean civil servants, Singapore, June 14, 1962.

35. Michael D. Barr, *Lee Kuan Yew: The Beliefs behind the Man* (Washington, D.C.: Georgetown University Press, 2000), p. 77.

36. Lee Kuan Yew, speech given at a rally in Klang, Singapore, April 16, 1964.

37. Lee Kuan Yew, speech given at the Imperial College Commemoration Eve Dinner, London, October 22, 2002.

38. Lee Kuan Yew, speech given at a dinner of the Foreign Correspondents Association, Tokyo, March 21, 1967.

39. Lee Kuan Yew, speech given at the annual dinner of the Singapore Employers' Federation, Singapore, May 10, 1968.

40. Speech by Minister Mentor Lee Kuan Yew at the Tanjong Pagar Chinese New Year Dinner, Singapore, February 10, 2006.

41. Lee Kuan Yew, "Asia, America, and Europe in the Next Millennium Towards Economic Complementarity and Convergence," speech given at the ABN-AMRO Symposium, June 6, 1997.

42. Lee Kuan Yew, speech given at the International Institute for Strategic Studies Conference, Singapore, September 12, 1997.

43. Plate, *Conversations with Lee Kuan Yew*, pp. 110–111.

44. Lee Kuan Yew, "Singapore-U.K. Relations: Bringing Forward an Old Friendship," speech given at the British Chamber of Commerce's 50th Anniversary Dinner, Singapore, January 8, 2004.

45. Lee Kuan Yew, "An Entrepreneurial Culture for Singapore," Ho Rih Hwa Leadership in Asia Public Lecture, Singapore, February 5, 2002.

46. Lee Kuan Yew, "For Third World Leaders: Hope or Despair?" Collins Family International Fellowship Lecture, Cambridge, Massachusetts, October 17, 2000.

47. Summary of a conversation between Lee Kuan Yew and John Thornton at the FutureChina Global Forum, Singapore, July 11, 2011.

48. Harvard University Leadership Roundtable with Lee Kuan Yew, "Personal Reflections on Leadership," Cambridge, Massachusetts, October 18, 2000.

49. Kwang et al., *Lee Kuan Yew: The Man and His Ideas*, p. 103.

50. Lee Kuan Yew, speech given at a meeting of the Consultation Youth and Leadership Training, Singapore, April 10, 1967.

51. Lee Kuan Yew, interview with Graham Allison and Robert D. Blackwill, March 28, 2012.

52. Han Fook Kwang, Zuraidah Ibrahim, Chua Mui Hoong, Lydia Lim, Ignatius Low, Rachel Lin, and Robin Chan, *Lee Kuan Yew: Hard Truths to Keep Singapore Going* (Singapore: Straits Times, 2011), pp. 389–390.

53. Lee Kuan Yew, eulogy at the state funeral service for Goh Keng Swee, Singapore, May 23, 2010.

54. Kwang et al., *Lee Kuan Yew: Hard Truths to Keep Singapore Going*, p. 390.
55. Lee Kuan Yew, interview with Mark Jacobson, July 6, 2009.
56. Seth Mydans, "Days of Reflection for the Man Who Defined Singapore," *New York Times*, September 11, 2010.

Belfer Center Studies in International Security

Published by The MIT Press

Sean M. Lynn-Jones and Steven E. Miller, series editors
Karen Motley, executive editor
Belfer Center for Science and International Affairs
John F. Kennedy School of Government, Harvard University

Acharya, Amitav, and Evelyn Goh, eds., *Reassessing Security Cooperation in the Asia-Pacific: Competition, Congruence, and Transformation* (2007)

Agha, Hussein, Shai Feldman, Ahmad Khalidi, and Zeev Schiff, *Track-II Diplomacy: Lessons from the Middle East* (2003)

Allison, Graham, and Robert D. Blackwill, with Ali Wyne, *Lee Kuan Yew: The Grand Master's Insights on China, the United States, and the World* (2012)

Allison, Graham T., Owen R. Coté Jr., Richard A. Falkenrath, and Steven E. Miller, *Avoiding Nuclear Anarchy: Containing the Threat of Loose Russian Nuclear Weapons and Fissile Material* (1996)

Allison, Graham T., and Kalypso Nicolaïdis, eds., *The Greek Paradox: Promise vs. Performance* (1997)

Arbatov, Alexei, Abram Chayes, Antonia Handler Chayes, and Lara Olson, eds., *Managing Conflict in the Former Soviet Union: Russian and American Perspectives* (1997)

Bennett, Andrew, *Condemned to Repetition? The Rise, Fall, and Reprise of Soviet-Russian Military Interventionism, 1973–1996* (1999)

Blackwill, Robert D., and Paul Dibb, eds., *America's Asian Alliances* (2000)

Blackwill, Robert D., and Michael Stürmer, eds., *Allies Divided: Transatlantic Policies for the Greater Middle East* (1997)

Blum, Gabriella, and Philip B. Heymann, *Laws, Outlaws, and Terrorists: Lessons from the War on Terrorism* (2010)

Brom, Shlomo, and Yiftah Shapir, eds., *The Middle East Military Balance, 1999–2000* (1999)

Brom, Shlomo, and Yiftah Shapir, eds., *The Middle East Military Balance, 2001–2002* (2002)

Brown, Michael E., ed., *The International Dimensions of Internal Conflict* (1996)

Brown, Michael E., and Sumit Ganguly, eds., *Fighting Words: Language Policy and Ethnic Relations in Asia* (2003)

Brown, Michael E., and Sumit Ganguly, eds., *Government Policies and Ethnic Relations in Asia and the Pacific* (1997)

Carter, Ashton B., and John P. White, eds., *Keeping the Edge: Managing Defense for the Future* (2001)

Chenoweth, Erica, and Adria Lawrence, eds., *Rethinking Violence: States and Non-State Actors in Conflict* (2010)

de Nevers, Renée, *Comrades No More: The Seeds of Change in Eastern Europe* (2003)

Elman, Colin, and Miriam Fendius Elman, eds., *Bridges and Boundaries: Historians, Political Scientists, and the Study of International Relations* (2001)

Elman, Colin, and Miriam Fendius Elman, eds., *Progress in International Relations Theory: Appraising the Field* (2003)

Elman, Miriam Fendius, ed., *Paths to Peace: Is Democracy the Answer?* (1997)

Falkenrath, Richard A., *Shaping Europe's Military Order: The Origins and Consequences of the CFE Treaty* (1995)

Falkenrath, Richard A., Robert D. Newman, and Bradley A. Thayer, *America's Achilles' Heel: Nuclear, Biological, and Chemical Terrorism and Covert Attack* (1998)

Feaver, Peter D., and Richard H. Kohn, eds., *Soldiers and Civilians: The Civil-Military Gap and American National Security* (2001)

Feldman, Shai, *Nuclear Weapons and Arms Control in the Middle East* (1996)

Feldman, Shai, and Yiftah Shapir, eds., *The Middle East Military Balance, 2000–2001* (2001)

Forsberg, Randall, ed., *The Arms Production Dilemma: Contraction and Restraint in the World Combat Aircraft Industry* (1994)

George, Alexander L., and Andrew Bennett, *Case Studies and Theory Development in the Social Sciences* (2005)

Gilroy, Curtis, and Cindy Williams, eds., *Service to Country: Personnel Policy and the Transformation of Western Militaries* (2007)

Hagerty, Devin. T., *The Consequences of Nuclear Proliferation: Lessons from South Asia* (1998)

Heymann, Philip B., *Terrorism and America: A Commonsense Strategy for a Democratic Society* (1998)

Heymann, Philip B., *Terrorism, Freedom, and Security: Winning without War* (2003)

Heymann, Philip B., and Juliette N. Kayyem, *Protecting Liberty in an Age of Terror* (2005)

Howitt, Arnold M., and Robyn L. Pangi, eds., *Countering Terrorism: Dimensions of Preparedness* (2003)

Hudson, Valerie M., and Andrea M. Den Boer, *Bare Branches: The Security Implications of Asia's Surplus Male Population* (2004)

Kayyem, Juliette N., and Robyn L. Pangi, eds., *First to Arrive: State and Local Responses to Terrorism* (2003)

Kokoshin, Andrei A., *Soviet Strategic Thought, 1917–91* (1998)

Lederberg, Joshua, ed., *Biological Weapons: Limiting the Threat* (1999)

Mansfield, Edward D., and Jack Snyder, *Electing to Fight: Why Emerging Democracies Go to War* (2005)

Martin, Lenore G., and Dimitris Keridis, eds., *The Future of Turkish Foreign Policy* (2004)

May, Ernest R., and Philip D. Zelikow, eds., *Dealing with Dictators: Dilemmas of U.S. Diplomacy and Intelligence Analysis, 1945–1990* (2007)

Phillips, David L., *Liberating Kosovo: Coercive Diplomacy and U.S. Intervention* (2012)

Shaffer, Brenda, *Borders and Brethren: Iran and the Challenge of Azerbaijani Identity* (2002)

Shaffer, Brenda, ed., *The Limits of Culture: Islam and Foreign Policy* (2006)

Shields, John M., and William C. Potter, eds., *Dismantling the Cold War: U.S. and NIS Perspectives on the Nunn-Lugar Cooperative Threat Reduction Program* (1997)

Tucker, Jonathan B., ed., *Toxic Terror: Assessing Terrorist Use of Chemical and Biological Weapons* (2000)

Utgoff, Victor A., ed., *The Coming Crisis: Nuclear Proliferation, U.S. Interests, and World Order* (2000)

Weiner, Sharon K., *Our Own Worst Enemy? Institutional Interests and the Proliferation of Nuclear Weapons Expertise* (2011)

Williams, Cindy, ed., *Filling the Ranks: Transforming the U.S. Military Personnel System* (2004)

Williams, Cindy, ed., *Holding the Line: U.S. Defense Alternatives for the 21st Century* (2001)

Belfer Center for Science and International Affairs

Graham Allison, Director
John F. Kennedy School of Government
Harvard University
79 JFK Street, Cambridge MA 02138
Tel: (617) 495-1400; Fax: (617) 495-8963
http://www.belfercenter.org belfer_center@hks.harvard.edu

The Belfer Center is the hub of the Harvard Kennedy School's research, teaching, and training in international security affairs, environmental and resource issues, and science and technology policy.

The Center has a dual mission: (1) to provide leadership in advancing policy-relevant knowledge about the most important challenges of international security and other critical issues where science, technology, environmental policy, and international affairs intersect; and (2) to prepare future generations of leaders for these arenas. Center researchers not only conduct scholarly research, but also develop prescriptions for policy reform. Faculty and fellows analyze global challenges from nuclear proliferation and terrorism to climate change and energy policy.

The Belfer Center's leadership begins with the recognition of science and technology as driving forces constantly transforming both the challenges we face and the opportunities for problem solving. Building on the vision of founder Paul Doty, the Center addresses serious global concerns by integrating insights and research of social scientists, natural scientists, technologists, and practitioners in government, diplomacy, the military, and business.

The heart of the Belfer Center is its resident research community of more than 150 scholars, including Harvard faculty, researchers, practitioners, and each year a new, international, interdisciplinary group of research fellows. Through publications and policy discussions, workshops, seminars, and conferences, the Center promotes innovative solutions to significant national and international challenges.

The Center's International Security Program, directed by Steven E. Miller, publishes the Belfer Center Studies in International Security, and sponsors and edits the quarterly journal *International Security*.

The Center is supported by an endowment established with funds from Robert and Renée Belfer, the Ford Foundation, and Harvard University, by foundation grants, by individual gifts, and by occasional government contracts.